THE ENGLISH NOVEL
FROM DICKENS TO LAWRENCE

By the same Author

*

CULTURE AND SOCIETY

THE LONG REVOLUTION

MODERN TRAGEDY

COMMUNICATIONS

DRAMA FROM IBSEN TO BRECHT
being a revised edition
of
DRAMA FROM IBSEN TO ELIOT

Novels

BORDER COUNTRY

SECOND GENERATION

THE ENGLISH NOVEL

From Dickens to Lawrence

RAYMOND WILLIAMS

Fellow of Jesus College,
Cambridge

NEW YORK
OXFORD UNIVERSITY PRESS
1970

PRINTED IN GREAT BRITAIN

CONTENTS

FOREWORD

This book is a record of a course of lectures on the novel from Dickens to Lawrence, which I have been giving for the last seven years in the English Faculty at Cambridge. At different times, there were eleven lectures, given in different combinations, and I have brought these together. The texts are based on verbatim notes and on some available transcripts.

R. W.

INTRODUCTION

I KEEP thinking about those twenty months, in 1847 and 1848, in which these novels were published: *Dombey and Son, Wuthering Heights, Vanity Fair, Jane Eyre, Mary Barton, Tancred, Town and Country, The Tenant of Wildfell Hall.*

What was it just then that emerged in England? It was of course no sudden process of just a few months. But we can see, looking back, those months as decisive. The English novel before then had its major achievements; it had Defoe and Fielding, Richardson and Jane Austen and Walter Scott. But now in the 1840s it had a new and major *generation*. For the next eighty years the novel was to be the major form in English literature. And this was unprecedented. What these months seem to mark above all is a new kind of consciousness, and we have to learn to see what this is, and some ways of relating it to the new and unprecedented civilisation in which it took shape.

The changes in society had been long in the making: the Industrial Revolution, the struggle for democracy, the growth of cities and towns. But these also, in the 1840s, reached a point of consciousness which was in its turn decisive. The twelve years from Dickens's first novel to his radically innovating *Dombey and Son* were also the years of the crisis of Chartism. The first industrial civilisation in the history of the world had come to a critical and defining stage. By the end of the 1840s the English were the first predominantly urban people in the long history of human societies. The institutions of an urban culture, from music-halls and popular Sunday newspapers to public parks museums and libraries, were all decisively established in these years. There was critical legislation on public health and on working-hours in factories. A major economic decision, on free trade and the repeal of the corn laws, had begun a long realignment of politics. In the struggle and disturbance of those years the future, of course, was not known. But the sense of crisis, of major and radical issues and decisions, was both acute and general. It is then not surprising that in just this decade a particular kind of literature—already known and widely read, but still not very highly regarded—should come to take on new life, a newly significant and relevant life. Here, in these hands, a generation of writers, in very different ways, found the common forms that mattered, in response to a new and varied but still common experience.

There were of course immediate and related reasons for the new importance of the novel. Reading of all kinds was increasing. Between the 1820s and 1860 the annual number of new books rose from 580 to over 2,600, and much of the increase was in novels. New methods of binding and printing had brought book-prices down. In the period in which these novels were published there were new cheap libraries: the Parlour and the Railway: not led, of course, by the new generation, but by others: Lytton, Marryat, G. P. R. James. The reading of newspapers and magazines was increasing rapidly, though the major period of expansion was still twenty years ahead. In every way the reading-public was still a minority, and the book-reading public especially so. But serial publication of fiction, in the new family magazines, was significantly expanding the number of readers of novels. Direct market factors were important to writers in more pressing and evident ways.

But this is no simple case, in the end, of demand and supply. Several of the best new writers were involved in the market, and with their eyes wide open to it: Dickens above all. But what was written and what had to be written had many other sources. The crisis of the society and the expansion of reading were themselves related. More and more people felt the need for this kind of knowledge and experience, as customary ways broke down or receded. But beyond even this, as we can see most clearly from the novels themselves, the new pressures and disturbances were not simple moulds out of which new forms came. The men and women who were writing—some at the centre of opinion-forming and the market, some distant and isolated—took from the disturbance of these years another impetus: a crisis of experience, often quite personally felt and endured, which when it emerged in novels was much more than a reaction to existing and acknowledged public features. It was a creative working, a discovery, often alone at the table; a transformation and innovation which composed a generation out of what seemed separate work and experience. It brought in new feelings, people, relationships; rhythms newly known, discovered, articulated; defining the society, rather than merely reflecting it; defining it in novels, which had each its own significant and particular life. It was not the society or its crisis which produced the novels. The society and the novels—our general names for those myriad and related primary activities— came from a pressing and varied experience which was not yet history; which had no new forms, no significant moments, until these were made and given by direct human actions.

What then can we define that emerged from those months: those twenty months in which, looking back, we can see so clearly a particular achievement: a confirmation of a generation; confirmation of a new importance, a new relevance and new forms? From the many possibilities in those varied reading experiences I would choose one bearing as central: the exploration of community: the substance and meaning of community.

From Dickens to Lawrence, over nearly a hundred years, this

bearing seems to me decisive. What community is, what it has been, what it might be; how community relates to individuals and relationships; how men and women, directly engaged, see within them or beyond them, for but more often against them, the shape of a society: these related themes are the dominant bearings. For this is a period in which what it means to live in a community is more uncertain, more critical, more disturbing as a question put both to societies and to persons than ever before in history. The underlying experiences of this powerful and transforming urban and industrial civilisation are of rapid and inescapable social change; of a newly visible and conscious history but at the same time, in most actual communities and in most actual lives, of a newly complicated and often newly obscure immediate process. These are not opposite poles: they are the defining characteristics of the change itself. People became more aware of great social and historical changes which altered not only outward forms—institutions and landscapes—but also inward feelings, experiences, self-definitions. These facts of change can be seen lying deep in almost every imagination.

And then of course it was right that the novel should be used to explore and to realise this process, in unprecedented ways. In the great eighteenth-century realists, in the precise social world of Jane Austen and in the historically conscious imagination of Scott, its powers and its possibilities were already evident. But though they drew some of their strength, their starting strength, from their great individual predecessors, these new novelists of a rapidly changing England had to create, from their own resources, forms adequate to the experience at the new and critical stage it had reached.

Two features of this development stand out. The historical novel, as Scott had developed it, has almost run its course—its fashionable course—before this generation began. Dickens used it occasionally; George Eliot went back to it once. But in the main line it had become a separate form: from history as change, eating into human consciousness, to history as spectacle, the spectacular past, as most clearly in Lytton. Each of these possibilities can be seen in Scott: the romantic use of the past to transcend the present had many colourful opportunities in fiction. But the permanent achievement of the romantic imagination, at the point of its deepest engagement with its own time, was not this kind of transcendence. It was the establishment of a position in human experience which was capable of judging—not incidentally but totally—the very society that was forming and changing it. Society from being a framework could be seen now as an agency, even an actor, a character. It could be seen and valued in and through persons: not as a framework in which they were defined; not as an aggregate of known relationships; but as an apparently independent organism, a character and an action like others. Society, now, was not just a code to measure, an institution to control, a standard to define or to change. It was a process that entered lives, to shape or to deform; a process personally known but then again suddenly distant, complex, incomprehensible, overwhelming.

In what had been learned of process in the historical novel, the new novel of social change—of the valuation of change—found its impetus, its initiative, its decisive and eagerly taken opportunity. Thomas Carlyle, who did more than anyone else in his generation to communicate this sense of history—of historical process as moral substance and challenge—came to think that the novel was outdated, that it could be replaced by history. He was of course to be proved wrong, but only by the transformation of the novel in very much the direction of his central argument. It was by becoming history, contemporary history—but a history of substance, of process, of the interaction

13

of public and private life—that one important kind of novel went to the heart of its time. When Balzac, in France, learned from Scott, he went back not to the Middle Ages, at a distance which was bound to be spectacle, but as Scott had done in his best work to the recent and connecting history of Scotland; to the decisive origin of his own epoch: to the years of the French Revolution. He learned in this way, in the search for origins, how to go on to write the continuing history of his time. The new English novelists learned in comparable ways: going back to the decisive origins of their own epoch, in the crises of the Industrial Revolution, of democratic reform and of the movement from country to town: from Charlotte Brontë on the Luddites in *Shirley* to George Eliot on the years before 1832 and on town and country in *Middlemarch* and in *Felix Holt*. It was in this kind of use of the historical imagination, rather than in the fanciful exercises of a *Romola* or a *Tale of Two Cities*, that the real growth took place. And it was in these ways that novelists learned to look, historically, at the crises of their own immediate time: at Chartism, at the industrial struggle, at debt and speculation, at the complicated inheritance of values and of property.

That was one very important line of development, but there is another, even more important, which enters even more deeply into the substance and form of the novel. Most novels are in some sense knowable communities. It is part of a traditional method—an underlying stance and approach—that the novelist offers to show people and their relationships in essentially knowable and communicable ways. Much of the confidence of this method depends on a particular kind of social confidence and experience. In its simplest form this amounts to saying—though at its most confident it did not have to be said— that the knowable and therefore known relationships compose and are part of a wholly known social structure, and that in and through the relationships the persons themselves can be wholly known. Thus from the middle term, of visible and comprehensible relationship, both societies and persons are knowable; indeed certain fundamental propositions about them can even be taken for granted, in terms of a received and mutually applicable social and moral code.

Many factors combined to destroy this confidence, in the process of extraordinary change through which the new novelists were living. One effect of this change has been widely recognised. It has indeed become a dogma—more properly, a half-truth—that persons are only partially knowable in and through relationships; that some part of the personality precedes and survives—is in a way unaffected by—relationships; that in this special sense persons are not knowable, are indeed fundamentally and crucially unknowable. And this is a belief which in itself forces new and very radical experiments in the novel; experiments which have been more active and more exclusive in every subsequent generation.

What is not so often recognised in this well-known effect is that at the other end of the scale a similar process has been evident: an increasing scepticism, disbelief, in the possibility of understanding society; a structurally similar certainty that relationships, knowable relationships, so far from composing a community or a society, are the positive experience that has to be *contrasted* with the ordinarily negative experience of the society as a whole (or of the society as opposed to the local and immediate community). An important split takes place between knowable relationships and an unknown, unknowable, overwhelming society. The full seriousness of this split and of its eventual consequences for the novel can be traced only towards the end of the century. But its pressure is evident from this first period of crisis: Dickens's response to it—a very early and major response—is perhaps the key to understanding him, and especially to understanding his very original and creative use of the novel as a form.

Now we have only to name this particular crisis—the crisis of the knowable community—to see how deeply it is related to the changes through which these novelists were living. We can see its obvious relation to the very rapidly increasing size and scale and complexity of communities: in the growth of towns and especially of cities and of a metropolis; in the increasing division and complexity of labour; in the altered and critical relations between and within social classes. In these simple and general senses, any assumption of a knowable community—a whole community, wholly knowable—becomes harder and harder to sustain. And we have to remember, with this, that there is a direct though very difficult relationship between the knowable community and the knowable person. Wordsworth, in *The Prelude*, had got through to this relationship very early. In the great seventh book—*Residence in London*—he directly related the new phenomenon of the urban crowd—not the occasional but the regular crowd, the new crowd of the metropolitan streets—to problems of self-identity, self-knowledge, self-possession:

> *How often in the overflowing Streets,*
> *Have I gone forward with the Crowd, and said*
> *Unto myself, the face of every one*
> *That passes by me is a mystery . . .*
> *. . . And all the ballast of familiar life,*
> *The present, and the past; hope, fear; all stays,*
> *All laws of acting, thinking, speaking man*
> *Went from me, neither knowing me, nor known.*

It is from this critical conjunction—the unknowable crowd and the unknowing and unknown individual—that he created the image of the blind beggar with the label telling his history and his identity:

It seemed
To me that in this Label was a type,
Or emblem, of the utmost that we know
Both of ourselves and of the universe.

It is a familiar romantic conclusion; but it is important that the insight occurred where it did: in the crowded street of a city. It is a related alienation, of a community and of persons, of the kind which Blake also had seen, with a sharper emphasis on power, in his poem *London*.

The problem of the knowable community, with its deep implications for the novelist, is then clearly a part of the social history of early nineteenth-century England and of the imaginative penetration and recoil which was the creative response. But what is knowable is not only a function of objects—of what is there to be known. It is also a function of subjects, of observers—of what is desired and what needs to be known. A knowable community, that is to say, is a matter of consciousness as well as of evident fact. Indeed it is to just this problem of knowing a community—of finding a position, a position convincingly experienced, from which community can begin to be known—that one of the major phases in the development of the novel must be related.

It is so often taken for granted that a country community, most typically a village, is an epitome of direct relationships: of face-to-face contacts, within which the novelist can find the substance of a fiction of personal relationships. Certainly this aspect of its difference from the city and the suburb is important. Most English novels before Dickens are centred in rural communities, and it is because he is centred in the city—and not only a city but a metropolis—that he has to find strength and basis in an alternative tradition: in the popular culture of urban industrial society. We shall see the measure of that change and his extraordinary creative use of it when we come to look at the substance of his fiction.

But even within rural communities the problem of what is known—what is desired and needs to be known—is very active and critical. This is the real key to a very important development of the country novel from Jane Austen to George Eliot and then again from George Eliot to Hardy. We shall trace this in detail, but it is worth now briefly looking back at the community of Jane Austen.

It is a truth universally acknowledged that Jane Austen chose to ignore the decisive historical events of her time. Where, it is still asked, are the Napoleonic wars: the real current of history? But history has many currents, and the social history of the landed families at that time in England was among the most important. As we sense its real processes we find that they are quite central and structural in Jane Austen's novels. All that prevents us from realising this is that familiar kind of retrospect, taking in Penshurst and Saxham and Buck's Head and Mansfield Park and Norland and even Poynton, in which all country houses and their families are seen as belonging effectively to a single tradition: that of the cultivated rural gentry. The continual making and remaking of these houses and their families is suppressed, in this view, by an idealising abstraction, and Jane Austen's world can then be taken for granted, even sometimes patronised as a rural backwater, as if it were a simple 'traditional' setting. And then if the social 'background' is in this sense settled, we can move to an emphasis on a fiction of purely personal relationships.

But such an emphasis is false, for it is not personal relationships, in the abstracted sense of an observed psychological process, that preoccupy Jane Austen. It is, rather, personal *conduct*: a testing and discovery of the standards which govern human behaviour in certain real situations. To the social considerations already implicit in the examination of conduct, with its strong sense and exploration of the adequacy of social norms, we must add from the evidence of the novels a direct preoccupation with estates incomes and social position, which are seen as indispensable elements of all the relationships that are projected and formed. Nor is this a preoccupation within a settled 'traditional' world; indeed much of the interest and many of the sources of the action in Jane Austen's novels lie in the changes of fortune—the facts of general change and of a certain mobility—which were affecting the landed families at this time.

Thus it would be easy to take Sir Thomas Bertram, in *Mansfield Park*, as an example of the old settled landed gentry to be contrasted with the new 'London' ways of the Crawfords (this is a common reading), were it not for the fact that Bertram is explicitly presented as what Goldsmith would have called 'a great West Indian': a colonial proprietor in the sugar island of Antigua. The Crawfords may have London ways, but the income to support them is landed property in Norfolk, and they have been brought up by an uncle who is an admiral. Sir Walter Elliot, in *Persuasion*, belongs to a landed family which had moved from Cheshire to Somerset and which had been raised to a baronetcy in the Restoration, but his income now will not support his position. His heir-presumptive has 'purchased independence by uniting himself to a rich woman of inferior birth', and the baronet is forced to let Kellynch Hall to an admiral since as his lawyer observes:

> this peace will be turning all our rich naval officers ashore. They will be all wanting a home. . . . Many a noble fortune has been made during the war.

The neighbouring Musgroves, the second landowning family, are by contrast in a state of alteration, perhaps of improvement. The father and mother were in the old English style, and the young people in the new.

Darcy, in *Pride and Prejudice*, is a landowner established for 'many generations' but his friend Bingley has inherited £100,000 and is looking for an estate to purchase. Sir William Lucas has risen from trade to a knighthood. Mr Bennett has £2,000 a year but an entailed estate, and has married the daughter of an attorney whose brother is in trade. Knightley, in *Emma*, owns Donwell Abbey, and Martin one of the new gentlemen farmers is his tenant. The Woodhouses have little land but Emma will inherit £30,000 'from other sources'. Elton the vicar has some independent property, but must 'make his way as he could, without any alliances but in trade'. Mr Weston belongs to a 'respectable family which for the last two or three generations has been rising into gentility and property'. He marries, through the militia, the daughter of 'a great Yorkshire family' and when she dies enters trade and purchases 'a little estate'. Harriet, finally revealed as the daughter of 'a tradesman, rich enough' marries her gentleman farmer with the reasonable 'hope of more, of security, stability, and improvement'. The Coles live quietly, on an income from trade, but when this improves 'in fortune and style of living, second only to the Woodhouses, in the immediate neighbourhood'. In *Sense and Sensibility* the Dashwoods are a settled landowning family, increasing their income by marriages, and enlarging the settlements of their daughters. They are also enclosing Norland Common, and buying up neighbouring farms; the necessary cashing of stocks for enclosure and engrossing affect the rate of the family's immediate improvement. In *Northanger Abbey*, Catherine Morland, the daughter of a clergyman with two good livings and a considerable independence, goes with a local landowning family, the Allens, to Bath, and in that sharply observed social exchange meets the son of the family which has owned the Abbey estates since the dissolution of the monasteries; his sister marries on the 'unexpected accession' of her lover 'to title and fortune'.

To abstract this social history is of course to describe only the world of the novels within which the more particular actions begin and end. Yet it must be clear that it is no single settled society. It is an active complicated sharply speculative process: of inherited and newly enclosing and engrossing estates; of fortunes from trade and colonial and military profit being converted into houses and property and social position; of settled and speculative marriages into estates and incomes. It is indeed that most difficult world to describe, in English social history: an acquisitive high bourgeois society at the point of its most evident interlocking with an agrarian capitalism that is itself mediated by inherited titles and by the making of family names. Into the long and complicated interaction of landed and trading capital, the process that Cobbett observed—the arrival of 'the nabobs, negro-drivers, admirals, generals' and so on—is directly inserted and is even taken for granted. The social confusions and contradictions of this complicated process are the true source of many of the problems of human conduct and valuation which the personal actions dramatise. An openly acquisitive society, which is concerned also with the *transmission* of wealth, is trying to judge itself at once by an inherited code and by the morality of improvement.

The paradox of Jane Austen is then the achievement of a unity of tone, of a settled and remarkably confident way of seeing and judging, in this chronicle of confusion and change. She is precise and candid, but in very particular ways. She is for example more exact about income, which is disposable, than about acres, which have to be worked. Yet at the same time she sees land in a way that she does not see 'other sources' of income.

Her eye for a house, for timber, for the details of improvement, is quick, accurate, monetary. Yet money of other kinds, from the trading houses, from the colonial plantations, has no visual equivalent; it has to be converted to these signs of order to be recognised at all. This way of seeing is especially representative. The land is seen primarily as an index of revenue and position; its visible order and control are a valued product but the process of working it is hardly seen at all. Jane Austen then reminds us, involuntarily, of the two meanings of improvement which were historically linked but in practice so often contradictory. There is the improvement of soil, stock, yields, in a working agriculture. And there is the improvement of houses, parks, artificial landscapes, which absorbed so much of the actually increasing wealth. It is the essential commentary on what can be abstracted technically as the agricultural revolution; that it was no revolution, but the consolidation the improvement and the expansion of an existing social class.

Cultivation has the same ambiguity as improvement. There is increasing growth and this is converted into rents, and then the rents are converted into what is seen as a cultivated society. What the 'revolution' is for, then, is this: this quality of life. Jane Austen could achieve her remarkable unity of tone—that cool and controlled observation which is the basis of her narrative method; that highly distanced management of event and description and character which need not become either open manipulation or participation and personal involvement—because of an effective formula: improvement is improvement. The working improvement, which is not seen at all, is the means of social improvement, which is then so isolated that it is seen very clearly indeed.

It is not seen flatteringly. The conversion of good income into good conduct was no automatic process. But what is crucial is that the moral pretension is taken so seriously that it becomes a critique: never of the basis of the formula, but coolly and determinedly of its results in character and action. She guides her heroines steadily to the right marriages. She makes settlements, alone, against all the odds, like some supernatural lawyer, in terms of that exact proportion to moral worth which could assure the continuity of the general formula. But within this conventional bearing, which is the source of her confidence, the moral discrimination is so insistent that it can be taken in effect as an independent value. It is said by literary historians that she derives from Fielding and from Richardson, but Fielding's genial manipulative bluff and Richardson's isolating fanaticism are in fact far back, in another world. What happens in *Emma*, in *Persuasion*, in *Mansfield Park*, is the development of an everyday uncompromising morality which is in effect separable from its social basis and which, in other hands, can be turned against it. It is in this sense that Jane Austen relates to those later writers who had to learn to assume, with increasing unease from Coleridge to George Eliot and Matthew Arnold, that there was no necessary correspondence between class and morality; that the survival of discrimination depended on another kind of independence; that the two meanings of improvement had to be not merely distinguished but contrasted; or, as first in Coleridge, that cultivation in its human sense had to be brought to bear as a standard *against* the social process of civilisation. In these hands, decisively, the formula broke down: improvement was not improvement; not only not necessarily but at times in definite contradiction. Jane Austen, it is clear, never went so far. Her novels would have been very different, involving new problems of structure and language, if she had. But she provided the emphasis which had only to be taken outside the park walls into a different social experience to become not a moral but a social criticism. It is this transformation and its difficulties that we shall meet in George Eliot.

But now consider again Jane Austen's 'knowable community'. It is outstandingly face-to-face; its crises, physically and spiritually, are in just these terms: a look, a gesture, a stare, a confrontation; and behind these, all the time, the novelist is watching, observing, physically recording and reflecting. That is the whole stance; the grammar of her morality. Yet while it is a community wholly known, within the essential terms of the novel, it is as an actual community very precisely selective. Neighbours in her novels are not the people actually living near by. They are the people living a little less near by who in social *recognition* can be visited. What she sees across the land is a network of propertied houses and families, and through this tightly drawn mesh most actual people are simply not seen. To be face-to-face in this world is already to belong to a class. No other community, in physical presence or in social reality, is by any means knowable. And it is not only most of the people who have disappeared. It is also most of the country, which becomes real only as it relates to the houses which are the real nodes. For the rest the country is weather or a place for a walk.

It is proper to trace the continuity of the novel—a very important tradition of moral analysis—from Jane Austen to George Eliot. But we can only do this intelligently if we recognise what else is happening in this literary development: a recognition of other kinds of people; other kinds of country; other kinds of action on which a moral emphasis must be brought to bear.

Thus *Adam Bede* is set by George Eliot in Jane Austen's period: at the turn of the eighteenth into the nineteenth century. What she sees is of course very different: not primarily because the *country* has changed, but because she is drawing on a different social tradition.

The germ of *Adam Bede* was an anecdote told me by my Methodist Aunt Samuel . . . an anecdote from her own experience. . . . I afterwards began to think of blending this and some other re-collections of my aunt in one story, with some points in my father's early life and character.

Thus the propertied house is still there, in the possession of the Donnithornes. But they are now seen at work on their income, dealing with their tenants:

'What a fine old kitchen this is!' said Mr Donnithorne, looking round admiringly. He always spoke in the same deliberate, well-chiselled, polite way, whether his words were sugary or veno-mous. 'And you keep it so exquisitely clean, Mrs Poyser. I like these premises, do you know, beyond any on the estate.'

We have encountered this 'deliberate, well-chiselled, polite' way of speaking before. But it is not now among relative equals, just as the old Squire's way of looking is not now simply an aspect of character but of character in a precise and domina-ting social relationship. As Mrs Poyser reacts to it:

'as if you was an insect, and he was going to dab his finger-nail on you'.

The proposition that is put through the politeness is in fact a reorganisation of the tenancy, for the estate's convenience, which will take away the Poysers' corn land. It is accompanied by a threat that the proposed new neighbour

'who is a man of some capital, would be glad to take both the farms, as they could be worked so well together. But I don't want to part with an old tenant like you'.

It is not a particularly dramatic event, but it is a crucial admission of everyday experience which had been there all the time, and which is now seen from an altered point of view. The politeness of improvement is necessarily counterpointed by the crude facts of economic power, and a different moral emphasis has become inevitable. This is then extended. The young squire is anxious to improve the estate; as the tenants saw it there was to be a millennial abundance of new gates, allowances of lime, and returns of ten per cent.

And he takes up Adam Bede as the manager of his woods. But in what is essentially the same spirit he takes up Hetty Sorrel as his girl and succeeds in ruining her. A way of using people for convenience is an aspect of personal character—this emphasis is not relaxed—but it is now also an aspect of particular social and economic relationships. And then as George Eliot observes ironically:

> it would be ridiculous to be prying and analytic in such cases, as if one was inquiring into the character of a confidential clerk. We use round, general, gentlemanly epithets about a young man of birth and fortune.

Jane Austen, precisely, had been prying and analytic, but into a limited group of people in their relations with each other. The analysis is now brought to bear without the class limitation. The social and economic relationships are seen necessarily as elements, often determining elements, of conduct.

The problem of the knowable community, that is to say, is not only a matter of physical expansion and complication. It is also and primarily a problem of viewpoint and of consciousness. And it is at this point, precisely, that it interlocks with the methods derived from the new historical consciousness; the new sense of society as not only the bearer but the active creator, the active destroyer, of the values of persons and relationships.

It is a complicated interaction. In the late 1830s and especially in the 1840s everything seems to start at once, in a quite newly experienced world. Between Jane Austen and Scott and the beginning of Dickens there is a pause, an interregnum: not in actual production, for the making of novels continued, and there are interesting isolated exercises, such as those of Peacock; but in vital contribution, in the making and remaking of a form and a generation. As we move to the 1840s we have to shift our attention this way and that, in so many new directions that no single account is possible. But before that decade there was this one decisive moment: the first appearance of Dickens. It took him many years, in and through his great success, to arrive at the works which now define his achievement. Yet it is not only the accident of time but this emphatic arrival of genius that directs our attention, from the beginnings in the 1830s, to Dickens: and above all to the Dickens who reached his full power and full difficulty as a novelist in those months of 1847 and 1848.

I

Charles Dickens

IT is still widely believed that the traditional culture of the English people was broken and disintegrated by the Industrial Revolution. What then emerged, it is said, was on the one hand a debased synthetic commercial culture—the world of the newspapers and popular entertainment; on the other hand an increasingly threatened minority culture—an educated tradition within which the finest literature and thought of the time sought to maintain and extend itself and to keep its connections, its continuities, with the best work of the past. Each of these descriptions seems to me partially true but when we have given them all the weight we can they still do not, taken together, describe the whole situation in urban and industrial England, and above all in its culture; in the novel especially. What is missing is that element of authentic popular response to the new conditions of life, through which in many ways—in new radical institutions and beliefs, but also in the crowded many-voiced anonymous world of idioms, stories, songs, jokes, parodies, sentiments, caricatures—people described and responded to their unprecedented experiences.

We do not yet know nearly enough about either of these kinds. The educated world has of course neglected them. In the last few years we have been getting some preliminary accounts: both of the radical culture which is so central an achievement, and in more fragmentary ways of the anonymous culture, which has a continuing, often oral, traditional strength. And as we begin to see these more clearly we can see the condition of literature in this rapidly changing society, and especially the condition of the novel, in some very new ways. We can especially realise our good fortune that at the most critical point in this history—at the time of the critical remaking of the novel and of the critical emergence of a new urban popular culture—we have a novelist of genius who is involved in both; we have Dickens.

The shift of emphasis involved here is of course very difficult. It extends its changes of viewpoint—some of them very radical—into a whole structure of critical and social beliefs. Dickens certainly is now more admired, more respected, more carefully studied than he has ever been, and especially within a minority critical public; the majority of readers he has of course always kept. But I do not think this would be happening in the way it now is if the other revaluation were not also going on, in what amounts to a recovery of some of the central history and culture of our own people: a history and a culture that had been excluded, set aside, by the rigidities of an old educated world. We are beginning to know now, with increasing substance and precision, our inherited popular culture; and to know its difference from a folk culture, which is perhaps the hardest point to grasp.

There are always eventual interactions, of a limited kind, between folk and polite culture. But characteristically each occurs in a relatively rigid and immobile society: in peasant communities and in courts; or in the country and in the city when these are relatively distinct. When the society becomes mobile, both internally and as a whole, these simpler kinds disappear in their old forms. Through many transitional stages we come to different cultures, where the terms that matter are not 'folk' and 'polite' (or 'aristocratic'); but significantly, 'popular' and 'educated'. In a class society of a modern kind these characteristically express a *relationship* rather than a distinction or separation. Thus when an 'educated' culture is called, as so often, a 'minority' culture, we have to see this as an indication of a social fact and relationship: the class limitation of education. 'Popular culture' is similarly a fact of the whole society, not of a distinct and separate area as in 'folk'.

Each kind of culture, in a class society, is aware of the other: involved, critical, responsive, hostile. And 'popular culture' is especially complicated, because it includes both what is provided *for* the majority and what is made *by* them. It would be simpler if these were wholly separable areas but as the whole history of fiction (among many other cases) indicates they are not and cannot be. When we say of Dickens that he draws on a popular culture, we do not mean that this is unaffected or that he is unaffected by the educated culture. Many serious ideas had been popularised, and there were earlier recognised artists who had expressed this popular life. No more can we say of George Eliot, who is the crucial contrasting case, that she draws on an educated culture (which is obviously true) but not on a popular culture (which especially in popular religion and rural life is as obviously part of her world). It is really the interaction, indeed the disturbance induced in her work by the changing relations between the 'educated' and 'popular' life and thought, that is decisive.

Similarly in popular culture, even before we get to Dickens's creative uses of it, we have to notice a range and a contradiction. It goes all the way from authentic popular response in idioms and values, through authentic popular demand for certain kinds of issue and story, through important earlier art and thought which had been based on or accepted into its sensibility, to exploitation and manipulation of popular response and demand (as in so much tendentious magazine fiction written to direct or deflect the interests of the majority) and finally to that most difficult area of all, in which certain adjustments, resignations, illusions, fantasies—born of the whole experience of the society—became popular and even self-generating. These are authentic enough in that they are widely represented, but they are also inauthentic in the sense that they are incapable of revealing, that they prevent others revealing, certain actual interests and truths. What is composed in particular (and this is very relevant to Dickens) is a self-defensive, alternately jolly or cynical tone and mood, which can take over and become very difficult to distinguish from the humorous or ironic popular observation of reality.

That is our central critical problem in Dickens. But it is masked by another which we had better deal with directly. By the standards of one kind of novel, which in England has been emphasised as the great tradition, Dickens's faults—what are seen as his faults—are so many and so central as to produce embarrassment. Almost every criterion of that other kind of novel—characteristically, the fiction of an educated minority—works against him. His characters are not 'rounded' and developing but 'flat' and emphatic. They are not slowly re-vealed but directly presented. Significance is not enacted in mainly tacit and intricate ways but is often directly presented in moral address and indeed exhortation. Instead of the con-trolled language of analysis and comprehension he uses, directly, the language of persuasion and display. His plots depend often on arbitrary coincidences, on sudden revelations and changes of heart. He offers not the details of psychological process but the finished articles: the social and psychological products.

Yet we get nowhere—critically nowhere—if we apply the standards of this kind of fiction to another and very different kind. We get nowhere if we try to salvage from Dickens what is compatible with that essentially alternative world, and then for the rest refer mildly and kindly to the great entertainer and to the popular tradition: not explaining but explaining away. The central case we have to make is that Dickens could write a new kind of novel—fiction uniquely capable of realising a new kind of reality—just because he shared with the new urban popular culture certain decisive experiences and responses. That he shared with it, also, certain adjustments and illusions is a significant but minor part of this case. Unless we acknowledge this new reality—essentially it is the reality of the new kind of city—we shall go on discussing his methods in abstract and marginal ways. Yet if we can grasp this new experience, we shall see how much of his method—his creative method—necessarily follows from it; that it is the only or at least the major way in which that unprecedented experience could be seen and valued; that it is a breakthrough in the novel from which those other novelists of cities—Dostoievsky and Kafka are the most immediate names—in their own ways learned. Not apology then. Not a slow resigned acceptance that he is not after all George Eliot. But emphasis—critical emphasis—that he is a new kind of novelist and that his method *is* his experience.

Of course we can acknowledge as a fact in itself his marvellous energy. But then the energy and the methods are in fact inseparable. It is through his very specific plots and characters and not in spite of them that he makes his intense and involving world. He takes and transforms certain traditional methods: not like George Eliot into more locally observed actions or more particularly known individuals or more carefully charted stages of growth of a relationship; but, in his own way, into a dramatic method which is uniquely capable of expressing the experience of living in cities.

As we stand and look back at a Dickens novel the general movement we remember—the decisive movement—is a hurrying seemingly random passing of men and women, each heard in some fixed phrase, seen in some fixed expression: a way of seeing men and women that belongs to the street. There is at first an absence of ordinary connection and development. These men and women do not so much relate as pass each other and then sometimes collide. Nor often in the ordinary way do they speak to each other. They speak at or past each other, each intent above all on defining through his words his own identity and reality; in fixed self-descriptions, in voices raised emphatically to be heard through and past other similar voices. But then as the action develops, unknown and un-acknowledged relationships, profound and decisive connections, definite and committing recognitions and avowals are as it were forced into consciousness. These are the real and inevitable relationships and connections, the necessary recognitions and avowals of any human society. But they are of a kind that are obscured, complicated, mystified, by the sheer rush and noise and miscellaneity of this new and complex social order.

This creation of consciousness—of recognitions and rela-tionships—seems to me indeed to be the purpose of Dickens's developed fiction. The need for it is at the centre of his social and personal vision:

Oh for a good spirit who would take the housetops off, with a more potent and benignant hand than the lame demon in the tale, and show a Christian people what dark shapes issue from amidst their homes, to swell the retinue of the Destroying Angel as he moves forth among them. For only one night's view of the pale phantoms rising from the scenes of our too long neglect; and from the thick and sullen air where Vice and Fever propagate together, raining the tremendous social retributions which are ever pouring down, and ever coming thicker. Bright and blest the morning that should rise on such a night; for men, delayed no more by stumbling-blocks of their own making, which are but specks of dust on the path between them and eternity, would then apply themselves, like creatures of one common origin, owning one duty to the Father of one family, and tending to one common end, to make the world a better place. Not the less bright and blest would that day be for rousing some who have never looked out upon the world of human life around them, to a knowledge of their own relation to it, and for making them acquainted with a perversion of nature in their own contracted sympathies and estimates; as great, and yet as natural in its development, when once begun, as the lowest degradation known. But no such day had ever dawned for Mr Dombey, or his wife; and the course of each was taken.

That potent and benignant hand, which takes off the housetops and shows the shapes and phantoms which arise from neglect and indifference; which clears the air so that people can see and acknowledge each other, overcoming that contraction of sympathy which is against nature: that hand is the hand of the novelist; it is Dickens seeing himself. And it's significant that this comes in a description of the city, in that same forty-seventh chapter of *Dombey and Son*. He is describing, in the image of a dense black cloud hanging over the city, the human and moral consequences of an indifferent and 'unnatural' society. It is an image to which he often returns: the obscurity, the darkness, the fog that keeps us from seeing each other clearly and from seeing the relation between ourselves and our actions, ourselves and others.

And this is another aspect of Dickens's originality. He is able to dramatise those social institutions and consequences which are not accessible to ordinary physical observation. He takes them and presents them as if they were persons or natural phenomena. Sometimes as the black cloud or as the fog through which people are groping and looking for each other. Sometimes as the Circumlocution Office, or Bleeding Heart Yard, where a way of life takes on physical shape. Sometimes as if they were human characters, like Shares in *Our Mutual Friend*, and of course the Great Expectations. This connects with his moral naming of characters: Gradgrind, McChoakumchild, Merdle. It connects also but in a less obvious way with a kind of observation which again belongs to the city: a perception, one might say, that the most evident inhabitants of cities are buildings, and that there is at once a connection and a confusion

34

between the shapes and appearance of buildings and the real shapes and appearances of the people who live in them.

As in this passage from *Little Dorrit*:

> Upon that establishment of state, the Merdle establishment in Harley Street, Cavendish Square, there was the shadow of no more common wall than the fronts of other establishments of state on the opposite side of the street. Like unexceptionable society, the opposing rows of houses in Harley Street were very grim with one another. Indeed, the mansions and their inhabitants were so much alike in that respect, that the people were often to be found drawn up on opposite sides of dinner-tables, in the shade of their own loftiness, staring at the other side of the way with the dullness of the houses.
>
> Everybody knows how like the street, the two dinner-rows of people who take their stand by the street will be. The expressionless uniform twenty houses, all to be knocked at and rung at in the same form, all approachable by the same dull steps, all fended off by the same pattern of railing, all with the same impracticable fire-escapes, the same inconvenient fixtures in their heads, and everything without exception to be taken at a high valuation—who has not dined with these? The house so drearily out of repair, the occasional bow-window, the stuccoed house, the newly-fronted house, the corner house with nothing but angular rooms, the house with the blinds always down, the house with the hatchment always up, the house where the collector has called for one quarter of an idea, and found nobody at home—who has not dined with these?
>
> The house that nobody will take, and is to be had a bargain— who does not know her? The showy house that was taken for life by the disappointed gentleman, and which does not suit him at all—who is unacquainted with that haunted habitation?

This is a formal description which takes the analogy of houses and people right through, and in the end playfully. But it recurs in more local insights, where the house and the life being lived in it are indistinguishable (this is again from *Little Dorrit*):

The debilitated old house in the city, wrapped in its mantle of soot, and leaning heavily on the crutches that had partaken of its decay and worn out with it, never knew a healthy or a cheerful interval, let what would betide. You should alike find rain, hail, frost and thaw lingering in that dismal enclosure, when they had vanished from other places; and as to snow, you should see it there for weeks, long after it had changed from yellow to black, slowly weeping away its grimy life. The place had no other adherents. As to street noises, the rumbling of wheels in the lane merely rushed in at the gateway in going past, and rushed out again: making the listening mistress Affery feel as if she were deaf, and recovered the sense of hearing by instantaneous flashes. So with whistling, singing, talking, laughing and all pleasant human sounds, they leaped the gap in a moment, and went upon their way.

Or again:

It was now summertime; a grey, hot, dusty evening. They rode to the top of Oxford Street, and there alighting, dived in among the great streets of melancholy stateliness, and the little streets that try to be as stately and succeed in being more melancholy, of which there is a labyrinth near Park Lane. Wildernesses of corner houses, with barbarous old porticoes and appurtenances, horrors that came into existence under some wrong-headed person in some wrong-headed time, still demanding the blind admiration of all ensuing generations and determined to do so until they tumbled down; frowned upon the twilight. Parasite little tenements, with the cramp in their whole frame, from the dwarf-hills in the mews, made the evening doleful. Rickety dwellings of undoubted fashion, but of a capacity to hold nothing comfortably except a dismal smell, looked like the last result of the great mansions breeding in-and-in; and, where their little supplementary bows and balconies were supported on thin iron columns, seemed to be scrofulously resting upon crutches. Here and there a Hatchment, with the whole science of Heraldry in it, loomed down upon the street, like an Archbishop discoursing on Vanity. The shops, few in number, made no show, for popular opinion was as nothing to them.

This method is very remarkable. It has its basis, of course, in certain properties of the language: perceptions of relations between persons and things. But in Dickens it is critical. It is a conscious way of seeing and showing. The city is shown as at once a social fact and a human landscape. What is dramatised in it is a very complex structure of feeling. Thus he can respond warmly to the miscellaneous bustle and colour of a mobile commercial life:

> Mr. Dombey's offices were in a court where there was an old-established stall of choice fruit at the corner: where perambulating merchants, of both sexes, offered for sale at any time between the hours of ten and five, slippers, pocket-books, sponges, dogs' collars, Windsor soap, and sometimes a pointer or an oil-painting.
>
> The pointer always came that way, with a view to the Stock Exchange, where a sporting taste (originating generally in bets of new hats) is much in vogue.

And it is characteristic that when Mr Dombey arrives none of these passing commodities is offered to him. His kind of trade, reflected in his house—his 'Home-Department'—has established itself in colder, more settled, more remote ways; and then another aspect of the city is evident:

> Mr. Dombey's house was a large one, on the shady side of a tall, dark, dreadfully genteel street in the region between Portland Place and Bryanstone Square. It was a corner house, with great wide areas containing cellars frowned upon by barred windows, and leered at by crooked-eyed doors leading to dust-bins. It was a house of dismal state, with a circular back to it, containing a whole suite of drawing-rooms looking up a gravelled yard, where two gaunt trees, with blackened trunks and branches, rattled rather than rustled, their leaves were so smoke-dried. The summer sun was never on the street, but in the morning about breakfast time, when it came with the water-carts and the old-clothes men, and the people with geraniums, and the umbrella-mender, and the man who trilled the little bell of the Dutch clock as he went along. It was soon gone again to return no more that day; and the bands of

music and the straggling Punch's shows going after it, left it a prey
to the most dismal of organs, and white mice; with now and then
a porcupine, to vary the entertainments; until the butlers whose
families were dining out, began to stand at the house-doors in the
twilight, and the lamp-lighter made his nightly failure in attempt-
ing to brighten up the street with gas. It was as blank a house inside
as outside.

The contrast between the dismal establishment and the strolling
variety of the streets is very clearly made. Again, the characteristics of houses and of people are consciously exchanged:

cellars frowned upon by barred windows, and leered at by
crooked-eyed doors.

This transposition of detail can then be extended, again with
some traditional support, to a way of seeing the city as a
destructive animal, a monster, utterly beyond the individual
human scale:

She often looked with compassion, at such a time, upon the
stragglers who came wandering into London, by the great high-
way hard by, and who, footsore and weary, and gazing fearfully
at the huge town before them, as if foreboding that their misery
there would be but as a drop of water in the sea, or as a grain of
sea-sand on the shore, went shrinking on, cowering before the
angry weather, and looking as if the very elements rejected them.
Day after day, such travellers crept past, but always, as she thought
in one direction—always towards the town. Swallowed up in one
phase or other of its immensity, towards which they seemed
impelled by a desperate fascination, they never returned. Food for
the hospitals, the churchyards, the prisons, the rivers, fever, madness, vice, and death—they passed on to the monster, roaring in
the distance, and were lost.

That is one way of seeing it: the rhetorical totalising view from
outside. But Dickens moves with still greater certainty into the
streets themselves: into that experience of the streets—the
crowd of strangers—which many of us now have got used to

but which in Blake and Wordsworth was seen as strange and threatening. Dickens recreates and extends this experience, in a new range of feeling, when Florence Dombey runs away from her father's dark house:

> The cheerful vista of the long street, burnished by the morning light, the sight of the blue sky and airy clouds, the vigorous freshness of the day, so flushed and rosy in its conquest of the night, awakened no responsive feelings in her so hurt bosom. Somewhere, anywhere, to hide her head! somewhere, anywhere, for refuge, never more to look upon the place from which she fled!
>
> But there were people going to and fro; there were opening shops, and servants at the doors of houses; there was the rising clash and roar of the day's struggle. Florence saw surprise and curiosity in the faces flitting past her; saw long shadows coming back upon the pavement; and heard voices that were strange to her asking her where she went, and what the matter was; and though these frightened her the more at first, and made her hurry on the faster, they did her the good service of recalling her in some degree to herself, and reminding her of the necessity of greater composure.
>
> Where to go? Still somewhere, anywhere! still going on; but where! She thought of the only other time she had been lost in the wide wilderness of London—though not lost as now—and went that way.

This street of the city is seen in very particular ways. It is a place of everyday business, not frightening in itself but amounting in its combined effect to a 'wide wilderness'. It is a place as difficult to relate to as her 'shut-up house'. But another note is struck: a physical effect which is also a social fact, sharply seen: the same social fact against which Dickens's effort at recognition and kindness is consistently made:

> the rising clash and roar of the day's struggle.

The only companion she finds is her dog, and she goes on with him:

With this last adherent, Florence hurried away in the advancing morning, and the strengthening sunshine, to the City. The roar soon grew more loud, the passengers more numerous, the shops more busy, until she was carried onward in a stream of life setting that way, and flowing, indifferently, past marts and mansions, prisons, churches, market-places, wealth, poverty, good, and evil, like the broad river side by side with it, awakened from its dreams of rushes, willows, and green moss, and rolling on, turbid and troubled, among the works and cares of men, to the deep sea.

What is emphatic here is not only the noise and the everyday business; not only the miscellaneity—'prisons, churches'; but through all this the indifference, in an unwilled general sense:

a stream of life setting that way, and flowing, indifferently.

It is again not a matter of particular acts or characters. It is a general phenomenon—a stream, a way of life. It is what Arthur Clennam and his wife go down into, in *Little Dorrit*, having learned, painfully, a precarious but still inviolable human connection:

They went quietly down into the roaring streets, inseparable and blessed; and as they passed along in sunshine and in shade, the noisy and the eager and the arrogant and the froward and the vain, fretted, and chafed, and made their usual uproar.

The individual moral qualities, still sharply seen, are heard as it were collectively, in the 'roaring streets'. This is again an advance in consciousness as it is very clearly a gain—now absorbed—in fictional method.

For we have to relate this view not simply to description—animated description—but to the power of dramatising a moral world in physical terms. The physical world is never in Dickens unconnected with man. It is of his making, his manufacture, his interpretation. That is why it matters so much what shape he has given it.

Dickens's method, in this, relates very precisely to his historical period. It was in just this capacity to remake the world, in the process we summarise as the Industrial Revolution, that men reached this crisis of choice; of the human shape that should underlie the physical creation. At one extreme Dickens can see this as comic:

> The earth was made for Dombey and Son to trade in, and the sun and moon were made to give them light. Rivers and seas were formed to float their ships; rainbows gave them promise of fair weather; winds blew for or against their enterprises; stars and planets circled in their orbits, to preserve inviolate a system of which they were the centre.

This is a mocking of a familiar commercial confidence but not at all in the name of an undisturbed nature. Rather it is a way of seeing the kind of system that is *imposed*, that is *made* central. It is qualified, precisely, by the other kinds of physical life and confidence in which men are making their own worlds, carrying them about with them through the noise and the crowding. It is not only that power is ambiguous—the power to create new worlds. There is also a choice: a choice of the human shape of the new physical environment. Or there *can* be a choice— we *can* be in a position to choose—if we see, physically and morally, what is happening to people in this time of unprecedented change:

> The first shock of a great earthquake had, just at that period, rent the whole neighbourhood to its centre. Traces of its course were visible on every side. Houses were knocked down; streets broken through and stopped; deep pits and trenches dug in the ground; enormous heaps of earth and clay thrown up; buildings that were undermined and shaking, propped by great beams of wood. Here, a chaos of carts, overthrown and jumbled together, lay topsy-turvy at the bottom of a steep unnatural hill; there, confused treasures of iron soaked and rusted in something that had accidentally become a pond. Everywhere were bridges that led nowhere; thoroughfares that were wholly impassable; Babel towers of chimneys, wanting half their height; temporary wooden

houses and enclosures, in the most unlikely situations; carcasses of ragged tenements, and fragments of unfinished walls and arches, and piles of scaffolding, and wildernesses of bricks, and giant forms of cranes, and tripods straddling above nothing. There were a hundred thousand shapes and substances of incompleteness, wildly mingled out of their places, upside down, burrowing in the earth, aspiring in the air, mouldering in the water and unintelligible as any dream. Hot springs and fiery eruptions, the usual attendants upon earthquakes, lent their contributions of confusion to the scene. Boiling water hissed and heaved within dilapidated walls; whence also, the glare and roar of flames came issuing forth; and mounds of ashes blocked up rights of way, and wholly changed the law and custom of the neighbourhood.

In short, the yet unfinished and unopened railroad was in progress; and from the very core of all this dire disorder, trailed smoothly away, upon its mighty course of civilisation and improvement.

This is the apprehension of direct disturbance, but Dickens goes on to see what in the end matters more: not the disorder of change, but the kind of new order that is made to emerge from it:

The miserable waste ground, where the refuse-matter had been heaped of yore, was swallowed up and gone; and in its frowsy stead were tiers of warehouses, crammed with rich goods and costly merchandise. The old by-streets now swarmed with passengers and vehicles of every kind; the new streets that had stopped disheartened in the mud and waggon-ruts, formed towns within themselves, originating wholesome comforts and conveniences belonging to themselves, and never tried nor thought of until they sprung into existence. Bridges that had led to nothing, led to villas, gardens, churches, healthy public walks. The carcasses of houses, and beginnings of new thoroughfares, had started off upon the line at steam's own speed, and shot away into the country in a monster train.

As to the neighbourhood which had hesitated to acknowledge the railroad in its struggling days, that had grown wise and penitent, as any Christian might in such a case, and now boasted of its powerful and prosperous relation. There were railway patterns in its drapers' shops, and railway journals in the windows of its newsmen. There were railway hotels, coffee-houses, lodging-houses, boarding-houses, railway plans, maps, views, wrappers, bottles, sandwich-boxes, and time-tables; railway hackney-coach and cabstands; railway omnibuses, railway streets and buildings, railway hangers-on and parasites, and flatterers out of all calculation. There was even railway time observed in clocks, as if the sun itself had given in. Among the vanquished was the master chimney-sweeper, whilom incredulous at Staggs's Gardens, who now lived in a stuccoed house three stories high, and gave himself out, with flourishes upon a varnished board, as contractor for the cleansing of railway chimneys by machinery.

To and from the heart of this great change, all day and night, throbbing currents rushed and returned, incessantly like its life's blood. Crowds of people and mountains of goods, departing and arriving scores upon scores of times in every four-and-twenty hours, produced a fermentation in the place that was always in action. The very houses seemed disposed to pack up and take trips. Wonderful Members of Parliament, who, little more than twenty years before, had made themselves merry with the wild railroad theories of engineers, and given them the liveliest rubs in cross-examination, went down into the north with their watches in their hands, and sent on messages before by the electric telegraph, to say that they were coming. Night and day the conquering engines rumbled at their distant work, or, advancing smoothly to their journey's end, and gliding like tame dragons into the allotted corners grooved out to the inch for their reception, stood bubbling and trembling there, making the walls quake, as if they were dilating with the secret knowledge of great powers yet unsuspected in them, and strong purposes not yet achieved.

The complexity of this feeling is a true complexity of insight. All the pride of power—the new power of the Industrial Revolution—is felt in the language: the circulation by railway is the 'life's blood'. But there is also the recognition of this power overriding all other human habits and purposes. It is the recognition confirmed, later, in

> the power that forced itself upon its iron way—its own—defiant of all paths and roads, piercing through the heart of every obstacle, and dragging living creatures of all classes, ages and degrees behind it.

The railway is at once the 'life's blood' and 'the triumphant monster, Death'. And in this dramatic enactment Dickens is responding to the real contradictions—the power for life or death; for disintegration, order and false order—of the new social and economic forces of his time. His concern always was to keep human recognition and human kindness alive, through these unprecedented changes and within this unrecognisably altered landscape.

> The very houses seemed disposed to pack up and take trips.

That is the mobility, the critical mobility, which was altering the novel. It is also the altered, the critically altered relationship between men and things.

In this altered relationship the character of moral analysis is inevitably changed. Thus it is easy to see that *Dombey and Son* is a novel about pride. But we have to go on and make a more difficult distinction. I suggested earlier that there is a kind of moral analysis in which society is a background against which the drama of personal virtues and vices is enacted, and that there is another kind—increasingly important in the development of nineteenth-century literature—in which society is the creator of virtues and vices; its active relationships and institutions at once generating and controlling, or failing to control, what in the earlier mode of analysis could be seen as faults of the soul.

And then the important thing to realise about a novel like *Dombey and Son* is that Dickens uses and relies on both these kinds. Indeed *Dombey and Son* is the novel in which he makes a decisive transition from the first to the second, in his essential organisation.

'I have dreamed,' said Edith in a low voice, 'of a pride that is all powerless for good, all powerful for evil; of a pride that has been galled and goaded, through many shameful years, and has never recoiled except upon itself; a pride that has debased its owner with the consciousness of deep humiliation, and never helped its owner boldly to resent it or avoid it, or to say, "This shall not be!" a pride that, rightly guided, might have led perhaps to better things, but which, misdirected and perverted, like all else belonging to the same possessor, has been self-contempt, mere hardihood, and ruin.'

She neither looked nor spoke to Florence now, but went on as if she were alone.

'I have dreamed,' she said, 'of such indifference and callousness, arising from this self-contempt; this wretched, inefficient, miserable pride; that it has gone on with listless steps even to the altar, yielding to the old, familiar, beckoning finger,—oh mother, oh mother!—while it spurned it; and willing to be hateful to itself for once and for all, rather than to be stung daily in some new form. Mean poor thing!

And now with gathering and darkening emotion, she looked as she had looked when Florence entered.

'And I have dreamed,' she said, 'that in a first late effort to achieve a purpose, it has been trodden on, and trodden down by a base foot, but turns and looks upon him. I have dreamed that it is wounded, hunted, set upon by dogs, but that it stands at bay, and will not yield; no, that it cannot, if it would; but that it is urged on to hate him, rise against him, and defy him!'

Her clenched hand tightened on the trembling arm she had in hers, and as she looked down on the alarmed and wondering face, her own subsided. 'Oh Florence!' she said, 'I think I have been nearly mad to-night!' and humbled her proud head upon her neck, and wept again.

That is a traditional kind of individualised moral description. In the same spirit there is a traditional invocation to wake from error, in the description of Florence going in to her father's room:

> Awake, unkind father! Awake now, sullen man! The time is flitting by; the hour is coming with an angry tread. Awake! Awake, doomed man, while she is near! The time is flitting by; the hour is coming with an angry tread; its foot is in the house, Awake!

But this is not the only way in which this destructive pride is seen. 'House' in this civilisation has two meanings: the family home and the firm. In bringing their values into contradiction, in the single word, Dickens sets going his characteristic conflict of primary and secondary feelings. For the outlook of the firm—a social institution, trading in the confident spirit of its time—is seen from the beginning as the creator of a destructively indifferent pride. Here, characteristically, Dickens does not plead emotionally, but sets down ironically:

> Common abbreviations took new meanings in his eyes, and had sole reference to them. A. D. had no concern with anno Domini, but stood for anno Dombei—and Son.

That is part of the observation—the satirical observation—that 'the earth was made for Dombey and Son to trade in'. It is the way in which social institutions, particular social purposes, reshape not only the physical but the moral world. And the question then arises: what is the nature, the human nature, by which this can be judged?

Was Mr. Dombey's master-vice, that ruled him so inexorably, an unnatural characteristic? It might be worth while sometimes, to inquire what Nature is, and how men work to change her, and whether, in the enforced distortions so produced, it is not natural to be unnatural. Coop any son or daughter to one idea, and foster it by servile worship of it on the part of the few timid or designing people standing round, and what is Nature to the willing captive who has never risen up upon the wings of a free mind—drooping and useless soon—to see her in her comprehensive truth!

Alas! are there so few things in the world, about us, most unnatural, and yet most natural in being so! Hear the magistrate or judge admonish the unnatural outcasts of society; unnatural in brutal habits, unnatural in want of decency, unnatural in losing and confounding all distinctions between good and evil; unnatural in ignorance, in vice, in recklessness, in contumacy, in mind, in looks, in everything. But follow the good clergyman, or doctor, who, with his life imperilled at every breath he draws, goes down into their dens, lying within the echoes of our carriage-wheels and daily tread upon the pavement stones. Look round upon the world of odious sights—millions of immortal creatures have no other world on earth—at the lightest mention of which humanity revolts, and dainty delicacy living in the next street, stops her ears, and lisps 'I don't believe it!' Breathe the polluted air, foul with every impurity that is poisonous to health and life; and have every sense, conferred upon our race for its delight and happiness, offended, sickened and disgusted, and made a channel by which misery and death alone can enter. Vainly attempt to think of any simple plant, or flower, or wholesome weed, that, set in this foetid bed, could have its natural growth, or put its little leaves forth to the sun as God designed it. And then, calling up some ghastly child, with stunted form and wicked face, hold forth on its un-natural sinfulness, and lament its being, so early, far away from Heaven—but think a little of its having been conceived, and born and bred, in Hell!

It is interesting to see where this question has led Dickens. Beginning with Dombey's 'master-vice', and its traditional reference to 'Nature', he has gone on to describe a process in which men work to change nature and to produce 'enforced distortions'. The argument then slips imperceptibly to the strongest social feeling he then had: his horror in seeing the diseased slums of the city, produced by indifference and neglect: a Hell produced and maintained by men.

It is at this point, significantly in the course of trying to answer a traditional moral question, that Dickens reaches not only an indignant social description but the definition of pur-pose that I have already quoted:

Oh for a good spirit who would take the house tops off

—a way of seeing through the 'dense black cloud'. An individual moral question has become a social question and then, decisively, a creative intervention. This seems to me the essential pattern of all Dickens's work.

What do we mean, precisely, by 'creative intervention'? What I mean, though it is hard to say, is that Dickens's morality, his social criticism, is in the form of his novels: a form based on ways of seeing people in their world and their society. Certainly these complicated ways of seeing are more important to his achievement than his separable attitudes to money, to poverty, to the family and to other known social questions. Nothing is clearer, when the treatment of any of these is examined by a method predicated by the assumption of 'treatment', than that Dickens is often contradictory, often confused, and indeed often, to use fashionable terms, unenlightened and unintelligent. And I do not mean that any of these observations is negligible, but they are only critical responses when they are parts of a whole response.

Thus it has been argued (and I among others have felt the force of this) that he is curiously blind to the real forces in nineteenth-century society which were even then beginning to 'reform the abuses against which he protested'. This is where an initial wrong assumption returns to confuse us. Certainly Dickens saw abuses and wanted them reformed. But it is not only that he increasingly saw them as related to a general condition: a fact reflected in the more concentrated organisation of the novels from *Dombey and Son* onwards. This was in the best sense an intellectual perception, and Shaw was right when he described it as 'declaring that it is not our disorder but our order that is horrible'.

More deeply, however, from his whole experience, and underlying the intellectual formulations which—like popular radical culture itself—he picked up from so many and so different and such contradictory sources, the total vision, not so much drawn from his material as imposed on it, came through and was decisive. This human drama, rooted and acted through, is inescapably general, and its generality, its totality, is its strength rather than its weakness. If the general condition and the forces operating on it were as he felt them to be, then what others may see as the 'real forces' can indeed seem incidental. Parliament, the trade unions, educational reform, public protective legislation of many kinds: outside the fiction Dickens can often see these as others saw them: now this opinion, now that. But the kinds of thing they were could not operate, at that level, in the fiction itself. We can say if we wish that this is blindness: an emotional overpowering of the ways in which the world has to be seen and changed. But it may be some check to our confidence, even now, to ask if the human and social condition as Dickens saw it has been much changed by the kind of work we call enlightened. The haunting isolation; the self-conscious neglect of the damned of the earth; the energy and despair of fixed public appearances, endlessly talking: these too are social facts and more resistible to reform than the institutions which they intersect.

To suppose that man as created by an immensely powerful society can be primarily affected by institutional amendments may not after all be very enlightened. This is why it is stupid of Orwell to dismiss Dickens as a 'change-of-heart' man (though it is characteristic of his own persistently external vision). Reference to a 'change of heart' is indeed now mainly known as a rationalisation of resistance to change, but this is clearly not Dickens. To see a change of heart and a change of institutions as alternatives is already to ratify an alienated society, for neither can be separated, or ever is, from the other; simply one or other can be *ignored*. The relevant question is still that of Marx: who educates the educators? Or, more generally, who legislates the legislators? Who mans the institutions?

In most important ways, Dickens has little in common with Marx. But they shared the sense of a general human condition:

> Human life is the true social life of man. As the irremediable exclusion from this life is much more complete, more unbearable, dreadful and contradictory, than the exclusion from political life, so is the ending of this exclusion, and even a limited reaction, a revolt against it, more fundamental, as man is more fundamental than the citizen, human life more than political life.

Marx is talking here of alienated labour but the vision is structurally similar to that of Dickens. Absolute human exclusion is more important than the relative kinds of exclusion which can be remedied by partial and piecemeal change. What Dickens saw as a redemption through love and innocence Marx saw as revolution, and that difference is crucial. But still, if this kind of total change is seen as the necessary response to a total condition, the consequent attitude to limited changes is governed by principle rather than by a kind of overlooking.

This is the key, surely, to Dickens's contradictions in the matter of character and environment. Consider this from *Nicholas Nickleby*:

> Now, when he thought how regularly things went on from day to day in the same unvarying round—how youth and beauty died, and ugly griping age lived tottering on—how crafty avarice grew rich, and manly honest hearts were poor and sad—how few they were who tenanted the stately houses, and how many those who lay in noisome pens, or rose each day and laid them down at night, and lived and died, father and son, mother and child, race upon race, and generation upon generation, without a home to shelter them or the energies of one single man directed to their aid—how in seeking, not a luxurious and splendid life, but the bare means of a most wretched and inadequate subsistence, there were women and children in that one town, divided into classes,

numbered and estimated as regularly as the noble families and folks of great degree, and reared from infancy to drive most criminal and dreadful trades—how ignorance was punished and never taught—how jail-door gaped and gallows loomed for thousands urged towards them by circumstances darkly curtaining their very cradles' heads, and but for which they might have earned their honest bread and lived in peace—how many died in soul, and had no chance of life—how many who could scarcely go astray, be they vicious as they would, turned haughtily from the crushed and stricken wretch who could scarce do otherwise, and who would have been a greater wonder had he or she done well, than even they, had they done ill—how much injustice, and misery and wrong, there was—and yet how the world rolled on from year to year, alike careless and indifferent, and no man seeking to remedy or redress it:—when he thought of all this, and selected from the mass the one slight case on which his thoughts were bent, he felt indeed that there was little ground for hope, and little cause or reason why it should not form an atom in the huge aggregate of distress and sorrow, and add one small and unimportant unit to swell the great amount.

This deliberately generalising description, which it pleases some people to call rant, is the general condition as Dickens quite consistently saw it. Within it, certainly, there is determinism: circumstances create evil. To that, inevitably, there is the humane response: help, where now no man seeks to 'remedy or redress'; teach, rather than punish, ignorance. But the whole description is of a *system*: the numbering into classes; the carelessness and indifference; the aggregate of distress and sorrow.

It is then a social condition but seen at a level where it is also a human condition. The complaint of beauty dying and ugliness surviving is what is so often now seen, by men who think they have outgrown social criticism, as 'criticising life'. But social criticism when it is most successful is always and inescapably a criticism of life. If Dickens believed that not only 'noisome pens' and 'stately houses' but the death of beauty and the 'griping' survival of ugliness were the products of the system, can we be quite sure that he was wrong? It would be easy to show him falling into confusion of unlike facts, in some 'general mood' of indignation. But death and survival, though they can be seen as absolutes, are almost always related to a general condition of living. And to push social criticism that far is to pass beyond what is ordinarily seen as social criticism but not to pass beyond social experience. Moreover, if the 'huge aggregate of distress and sorrow' is seen as a human condition, in this way of living, it is seen as a matter for response rather than for mere recognition. Nicholas, after this vision, 'gradually summoned up his utmost energy'. It is what Dickens manages to do, almost always, by way of intervening. He often believed because he must try to believe that good circumstances would produce good characters, and so help for the unfortunate. But already, in this early novel, he cannot see it as a *general* fact. The comfortable turn haughtily away, and from *Dombey and Son* onwards we see a social system in which the turning away is as much a product of circumstances as the distress. Indifference indeed, in the later novels, is a thing that the system and its expectations actively teach.

Yet under the weight of this system, and from no demonstrable cause, a turning towards also occurs. It is easy to show that having defined a social condition as the cause of virtue and vice, Dickens then produces virtue, almost magically as in *Little Dorrit*, from the same conditions which in others bred vice; or produces charity by making an exceptional and surprising benevolence flourish, overriding the determinism of the system, or often by an arranged and unexplained withdrawal from the system, where charity can suddenly be afforded.

We may or may not believe in it, as social observation, but though it has the character of miracle it is the kind of miracle that happens: the flowering of love or energy which is inexplicable by the ways of describing people to which (usually under the influence of the same system) we have got used. There is no reason, that is to say, for love or innocence, except that almost obliterated by this general condition there is humanity. The exclusion of the human, which we can see operating in a describable system, is not after all absolute, or it would make no sense to call what is alienated human; there would otherwise be nothing to alienate. The inexplicable quality of the indestructible innocence, of the miraculously intervening goodness, on which Dickens so much depends and which has been casually written off as sentimentality is genuine *because* it is inexplicable. What is explicable, after all, is the system, which consciously or unconsciously has been made. To believe that a human spirit exists, ultimately more powerful than even this system, is an act of faith but an act of faith in ourselves. That this became more and more difficult for Dickens is not surprising, but to the end, under increasing pressure, it is what he is not only saying but making happen.

It is in this dimension that we must judge his creation of characters. There has been an important critical difficulty about what is called his reduction of people to caricatures and about what is called the 'sentimentality' of his 'impossibly pure' heroines. But Dickens was creating, openly and deliberately, a world in which people had been deprived of any customary identity and yet in which, paradoxically, the deprivation was a kind of liberation, in which the most fantastic and idiosyncratic kinds of growth could come about. People had to define themselves and their position in the world—it is his characteristic mode:

'My present salary, Miss Summerson, at Kenge and Carboy's, is two pound a week. When I first had the happiness of looking upon you, it was one-fifteen, and had stood at that figure for a lengthened period. A rise of five has since taken place, and a further rise of five is guaranteed at the expiration of a term not exceeding twelve months from the present date.'

'When I offered to your sister to keep company, and to be asked in church, at such times as she was willing and ready to come to the forge, I said to her, "And bring the poor little child. God bless the poor little child".'

'But that's like me I run away with an idea and having none to spare I keep it, alas there was a time dear Arthur that is to say decidedly not dear nor Arthur neither but you understand me when one bright idea gilded the what's-his name horizon of et cetera but it is darkly clouded now and all is over.'

'My friends, what is this which we now behold as being spread before us? Refreshment. Do we need refreshment then, my friends? We do. And why do we need refreshment, my friends? Because we are but mortal, because we are but sinful, because we are but of the earth, because we are not of the air. Can we fly, my friends? We cannot. Why can we not fly, my friends?'

The emphasis is often isolated, often absurd, but what runs through it is a paradoxical energy. It is a loss of customary settlement, though not of customary phrases, which in their abstract repetition can become ludicrous because misplaced. But at the same time it is a kind of release, which even at its most grotesque is irrepressible and above all various. It is in this paradoxical dimension that Dickens creates the ordinary human condition, in ways that are clearer and sharper, given his general vision, than any more normative characterisation could be. Many of the techniques for this kind of description came from popular journalism, including 'police characters', from popular illustrations and cartoons, and from the theatre. It is from the theatre also and especially from melodrama that the counterweight is taken: the stabilising simple figures of innocence and purity. These are not the morality figures of an age of common belief, but the dramatic figures of an age in which individuality and growth are paradoxical and in which, as an emphasis and an intervention, the simplest human qualities of love and kindness must be deliberately sustained. It is a structure of feeling, in its strengths and weaknesses, which he shares with the popular culture of his time.

At the same time, by moving this structure into an extended action, Dickens ran into problems which are quite specific to his own art. There are times when the emotions can seem too large for the objects and situations through which they are released, and the line between intensity and absurdity is then often crossed, quite apart from those occasions when the dramatic structure fails, temporarily, to hold and is merely remembered and imitated. Where the failure is in the writing we can only note and consider it. But when there is overlapping of meaning it may be possible to avoid some of our own failures by analysis. Here is a mixed case:

> The mature young gentleman is a gentleman of property. He invests his property. He goes in a condescending amateurish way, into the City, attends meetings of directors, and has to do with traffic in Shares. As is well known to the wise in their generation, traffic in Shares is the one thing to have to do with in this world. Have no antecedents, no established character, no cultivation, no ideas, no manners; have Shares. Have Shares enough to be on Boards of Direction in capital letters, oscillate on mysterious business between London and Paris, and be great. Where does he come from? Shares. Has he any principles? Shares. What squeezes him into Parliament? Shares. Perhaps he never of himself achieved success in anything, never originated anything, never produced anything. Sufficient answer to all: Shares. O mighty Shares!

It is true that this passage would have 'special force in the years just before the crisis of 1866, which saw the failure of Overend and Gurney', and that it is integrated into the novel by its reference to the careers of several of the characters. But we do not need to deny these points to remind ourselves that this power of making an abstraction into a dramatic force is, as we have seen, a major element in all Dickens's social vision. And it is just here that the problem of 'exaggeration' is hardest. Traffic in shares is the *one* thing to have to do with the world? Do even the wise in their generation believe that? It is like 'no man seeking to remedy or redress it', in the *Nickleby* passage, when the most casual observation would have turned up a thousand. Is Dickens then being unfair? Is such a character credible?

But the character here is Shares. And the question is not really whether share capital, as a technique, leads to economic prosperity or to the crash of Overend and Gurney. It is what quality of living, what kinds of relationships, Shares embody (the repeated capital letter is important, as is stressed again in 'Boards of Direction'). It is not so much an isolated economic technique or an isolated aspect of character. It is more a free-acting force, separated from man though of course created by him. That it then in turns creates behaviour, principles, power: this is the whole point and the social observation is indeed fundamental—this is a *general* condition. The dramatic element, which Shares becomes, is like the dust-heaps and the river and the isolated colliding characters who live through and on them and who are brought to a willed and valued resolution. If you ask in detail how shares operate, this share and that, or how and why businesses flourish and fall, you are outside the drama, but what you have gained in one kind of contact with reality you have lost in another: learning the detailed workings but missing Dickens's dramatisation of what he saw as the total experience.

And this is of course very easy to do, quite apart from Overend and Gurney. For once he has got his dramatic figure, Dickens literally throws the book at it. The received phrases of aristocratic values—'antecedents, established character, cultivation, ideas, manners'—are hurled with the bourgeois values—

'achieved success, originated, produced'. Are these then to be set against Shares? Is that Dickens's meaning? But then which set of values, or both? From the primary feeling—that shares are replacing men as the active creators of the world—there is a rapid process of translation and overlapping, through the ordinarily available meanings. It is like the spectre attendant on Merdle addressing the high priests of the Circumlocution Office—'Are such the signs you trust and love to honour; this head, these eyes, this mode of speech, the tone and manner of this man?', for all the world as if it were Matthew Arnold. The spectre is the general vision; the words are from the book. And in a sense, any book will do, once the action is joined. Mainly Carlyle, of course, and the angry, sarcastic radicalism of Cobbett. But also, when it can help, a proposition about utility (as House has shown); a constructive suggestion from Robert Owen (character immediately alterable by change of circumstances); an appeal for organised charity and a tirade against it; a reminiscence of Scripture; a detail from a contemporary report; a statistic and a tirade against statistics. It wouldn't be difficult, picking up all these bits and pieces and seeing how often they are contradictory, to call Dickens merely irresponsible; indeed it has been done. But the responsibility, finally, is to the general vision, and in the end this is deep and remarkable. At the surface, there is the confusion of theory and the debris of phrases so characteristic of this period of English popular radicalism; and that the confusion persisted, that Dickens even propagated it, is historically very important. But still, the whole drama of values, the powerful way of seeing the world so that it cannot but be criticised and responded to: these, as substance, are more penetrating into the reality of nineteenth-century England than any of the systems which were in fact made clear and consistent.

Even the deepest contradictions are within this power. The

vision of alienation has its own alienated elements: a child is destroyed, as in *Dombey and Son*, by the subjection of a human being to a social role, but then Toodles or Cuttle are similarly subjected, by their author, who defines their whole reality in the jargon of their job, not only to show but in fact to minimise the pressures on them. The appeasing ventriloquism of the whining poor is only a step from the desperate inarticulacy of men subject to arbitrary economic power, but the step is taken. The aggregate of distress and sorrow has only to move, collectively, to be converted into its opposite and be seen as a howling mob. The trick played by Dombey on Polly, making her Richards for his convenience, is played by Meagles on Tattycoram, but the flow of feeling is now different. The good are *our* people, even when other people are different only because they are minor characters. Money corrupts, but it does not corrupt Sol Gills. The house of Dombey deserves to fall, but Walter can re-establish it. There are very many examples of this kind. The hurling of random ideas and the profoundly selective character of the moral action have certainly to be recognised. They are the problems of translation, but also the probable accompaniments of so single, intense, compulsive and self-involving a vision: the characteristic weaknesses where we have already recognised the strengths.

But the social criticism, giving that phrase its full value—not a set of opinions only, nor a series of reforms only, nor even habitual attitudes only, but a vision of the nature of man and the means of his liberation in a close and particular place and time—this social criticism is in the end marvellously achieved and still profoundly active. For indeed it is the kind of social criticism which belongs to literature and especially, in our own civilisation, to the novel. Sociology can describe social conditions more accurately, at the level of ordinary measurement. A political programme can offer more precise remedies, at the level of ordinary action. Literature can attempt to follow these modes, but at its most important its process is different and yet still inescapably social: a whole way of seeing that is communicable to others, and a dramatisation of values that becomes an action.

II

Charlotte and Emily Brontë

IT is some indication of the originality of those twenty
months in 1847 and 1848 that two novels should come out
as different from Dickens and from each other as *Jane Eyre* and
Wuthering Heights. Since Charlotte and Emily were sisters the
novels have always been linked in a general way, and there is
something else, more specific, that links them: an emphasis on
intense feeling, a commitment to what we must directly call
passion, that is in itself very new in the English novel. In the
end the critical interest is how different the novels are, what a
radical difference of method each shows and sustains. But as a
first emphasis the intensity of the feeling is decisive.

And this belongs, I think, in the moving earth, the unprecedented disturbance of those English years. Later, much later,
by a process we shall trace, it was possible to set what was
called social criticism against what was called psychology, or a
response to poverty and oppression against a response to the
intensities and difficulties of love and growth. On that later
projection the interests of the Brontë sisters and the interests of
Dickens and Elizabeth Gaskell are in different continents, the
East and West of society and personality. But in experience and
in these novels it is not like that. The world we need to remember if we are to see these connections of the 1840s is the world
of Blake: a world of desire and hunger, of rebellion and of
pallid convention: the terms of desire and fulfilment and the
terms of oppression and deprivation profoundly connected in a
single dimension of experience.

Nobody later achieves Blake's kind of unity; he could only

barely maintain it himself. But I think we need to start from the feeling, the central feeling, that an intensity of desire is as much a response, a deciding response, to the human crisis of that time as the more obviously recognisable political radicalism. Indeed, to give that kind of value to human longing and need, to that absolute emphasis on commitment to another, the absolute love of the being of another, is to clash as sharply with the emerging system, the emerging priorities, as in any assault on material poverty. What was at issue really was relationship itself: a dimension of relationship made problematic and dangerous by the increasing pressure, the external and internal and continuing pressure, to reshape, to deform—it is how Blake saw it—this most human, most absolute experience.

An affirming emphasis had been powerfully there in the greatest Romantic poems. And the significance of this emphasis is that it connects, structurally, what seem very different feelings: an intense affirmation of love and desire and an intense often desperate apprehension of isolation and loss. For a number of reasons this was slow to enter the novel. A certain worldliness, readily understandable in earlier periods (though never, I think, as persuasive as is made out), made for the qualification of love; found its value as social exchange and respect, as most coolly in Jane Austen; or its value as a factor, an isolable factor, in orthodox romance. What was directly expressed in Blake and in Keats and in different ways in Shelley and Byron seems to have gone underground, before the 1840s, in fiction and even in drama; indeed is literally underground in the dark images of the Gothic and in the produced straining extravagances of melodrama. The achievement of the Brontë sisters, before we say anything else, is that in different ways they remade the novel so that this kind of passion could be directly communicated.

There are precedents certainly: precedents as elements of

these new forms. The fire and madness of romance; the apparitions and dreams of the Gothic: these isolable elements can of course be picked up, are still often picked up to push *Jane Eyre* or *Wuthering Heights* into a familiar tradition. But then we have also to ask what the achieved social mode, social tone, in itself excluded. Especially if we remember that in a more evidently powered society it was a masculine mode. I don't mean universally or generically masculine, but what manly was coming to mean. It's a difficult point now, in public, but it has always seemed to me significant that through this mid-nineteenth century, through a process of alteration of feeling, of acknowledgeable feeling, which especially in the new public schools found its confident training institutions, men learned not to cry, I mean not to show themselves crying (even the word, this late, has a defensive laugh near it, standing guard). Within two generations not only the convention but perhaps the impulse had changed. What was taught and learned was a new and rigid control, 'self-control'—even weak men not crying and being very stiff and proud of it where much stronger men before them had quite openly wept when the feeling, the impulse was there. It's only one point among many: the new rigidity, public soberness of dress—men and women—is I think related. And in this tightening world it's then significant, surely, how much was kept alive, how much was newly affirmed, by a group of women novelists—by Elizabeth Gaskell, by Charlotte and Emily and Anne Brontë, and by—but see how the convention bore down—by Currer and Ellis and Acton Bell, by Marian Evans becoming George Eliot. That tension, I think, can never at all be forgotten. And it isn't only, to use the terms of the change, keeping a woman's world going. On the contrary: in certain vital ways simply a human world.

But that they were also women had another effect. People still have to fight past the governess to get to the Brontë sisters.

I mean fight past the image, the depressing image, that is still taken for granted. Before women could be educated, in anything like equal ways, it was there girls went if they had the start of an education but not enough private income: the women teachers, the woman intellectuals, and I don't doubt others, of later and different periods. Seen from the middle-class way round, and especially from the male middle-class way, the governess as a figure is repressive, unfeminine, dowdy. But I'd follow those girls through, pushed out as they were into one of the only available jobs, follow Jane Eyre and Lucy Snowe to Sue Bridehead in Hardy or Ursula Brangwen in Lawrence; or beyond them, even more, to Tess and to Miriam. I don't know how much I now need to insist on breaking the image: that deforming image which obscures—and is meant to obscure—a particular and a general repression. But at least we must say that the Brontë sisters knew directly a whole structure of repression in their time; knew it and in their own ways broke it with a strength and a courage that puts us all in their debt.

In their own ways broke it: that's where we must concentrate. The power and intensity of *Wuthering Heights* need no additional emphasis. The recognition has been given. The control of *Wuthering Heights*, the equally remarkable control, is now also quite generally acknowledged. And the power of *Jane Eyre* and of *Villette* needs no further adjectives. Readers still respond to the novels and critics follow them; sometimes critic following reader a bit uneasily in the same personality. What I mainly want to say is concerned with the differences between the novelists: differences that are profoundly important in the subsequent history. And then take *Wuthering Heights* first, for there it might seem is a novel without a history: a novel without precedents or descendants.

Its structure indeed is unique, though in spirit it is in no way isolated; it belongs in an English tradition with Blake and Lawrence and very specifically with Hardy. What is most remarkable about it, though, as a form is its exceptional fusion of intensity and control. No novel in English contains more intense and passionate feeling, but contains, then, is a word to consider. What we most remember from the novel, the passion of Cathy and Heathcliff, is in its actual creation very precisely, very consciously inset, qualified, modulated. The multiple narrative through secondary characters, the complications of the time-scheme, the precision of the complicated plot of inheritance and generations are so deliberate, so measured, and the staple of their language so consciously formal—in so many different ways formal, among the roughness, the plainness, of so much of the speech and the life—that we know in reading an extraordinary and intricate tension; and even when we know it are surprised, looking back, to find how large a proportion of the novel—in quantity and emphasis—is this measuring, qualifying, consequential narrative. Only an abstracted version of the single intense theme could support the still common description of extravagance, whether approved or disapproved. Yet this theme itself is so profoundly insistent that the novel refuses to be reduced to the sum of its other parts. Its interaction, its extraordinary intricacy of opposed and moderated but still absolute feelings, is an active, dynamic process: not balance but dialectic: contraries.

Seeing part of this, some critics have turned the discussion, rightly turned it, from the ordinary terms of romance—or from the more extreme emphases of the mystical and the melodramatic—and located *Wuthering Heights* in a social history. And it is certainly true that the Brontës lived in a border country, on the empty moors near a new and disturbed industrial area. Charlotte used this experience directly in *Shirley*, though backdating its events to the Luddites. And it has been

argued that this same disturbance—the new industrial dislocation, the birth of an outcast class, dark, unprecedented and
exposed—is at the root of *Wuthering Heights*; even, as has been
said, that Heathcliff is the proletariat. But social experience,
just because it is social, does not have to appear in any way
exclusively in these overt public forms. In its very quality as
social reality it penetrates, is already at the roots of, relationships of every kind. We need not look only, in a transforming
history, for direct or public historical event and response. When
there is real dislocation it does not have to appear in a strike or
in machine-breaking. It can appear as radically and as authenti-
cally in what is apparently, what is actually personal or family
experience. Any direct reference of *Wuthering Heights* to that
transforming social crisis seems to me then displaced, for this
exact reason: that its real social experience is then explicitly
reduced.

The same is true, I would say, of that closer reading, not
symbolic displacement but a kind of naturalist extension. Thus
it is certainly clear that the contrast between the Heights and
the Grange *is* a conscious contrast between two kinds of life:
an exposed unaccommodated wrenching of living from the
heath, and a sheltered refined civilised and *rentier* settlement in
the valley. We don't have to force this: it is directly rendered
when Heathcliff and Cathy look in on the Lintons and at many
other points in the complicated journeys—the connected personal and social moves—between the two houses. But this
social experience is the condition within which a more precise
and more searching action occurs and is measured, and there
is no convincing way in which the context—the real social
description—can be made to override the direct and preoccupying relations between persons. What we have again to
say is that social experience is a whole experience. Its descriptive
or analytic features have no priority over its direct realisation

in quite physical and specific personal feelings and actions. Without the central relationships, the physical and social landscape of *Wuthering Heights* would be a country waiting to be entered, waiting to be understood, for all its careful detail. What makes it a human landscape is that specific people with specific desires live and relate there.

We can not then draw back from that immediate and intricate experience, as either the symbolist or the naturalist mode would involve. Yet the central experience is at first sight so strange that there is some obvious anxiety, from conventional positions.

> If all else perished, and *he* remained, *I* should still continue to be; and if all else remained, and he were annihilated, the universe would turn to a mighty stranger: I should not seem a part of it. My love for Linton is like the foliage in the woods: time will change it, I'm well aware, as winter changes the trees. My love for Heathcliff resembles the eternal rocks beneath: a source of little visible delight, but necessary.

These words of Cathy have been called mystical, or a romantic extravagance. But I don't know how that can be said if we listen and follow the action. That kind of bond, that sense of absolute presence, absolute existence in another, in one another, is indeed an ordinary though of course always a transforming experience. In many lives, again and again, it is the central reality of everything else that happens, and indeed quite often doesn't need to be emphasised: the reality of the relationship is simply there and unbreakable.

In *Wuthering Heights* what has most to be said is that Cathy's affirmation is a matter of reality but that in her very statement of it, at that point in the action, something is being denied as well as affirmed. What happens really is that this central affirmation—not desire *for* another but desire *in* another; a depth of relationship around which an idea of oneself and literally then of the universe forms—is both stated and taken for granted: and the taking for granted is the profound, the dislocating error. 'A source of little visible delight, but necessary': but if it is necessary it can't be assumed or taken for granted, however deep it may lie. It has to be lived. Everything, literally everything, has to be lived in its light. It is a reciprocated feeling, literally a relationship: that kind of relationship which is truly given rather than taken, which is there and absolute before anything else can be said. In its quality as given—here in a childhood, a shared childhood in a place—it is where social and personal, one's self and others, grow from a single root.

And it is then a terrible blasphemy but also a real process—a social and historical process in a life and in a time—when the necessary is seen as so deep that under pressure, under pressure from other people, other ways, it is taken for granted; when on other bearings or in a different light it is in effect set aside so that another sort of reality—indeed an apparently desirable reality—can be attempted and made.

Cathy, specifically, marries Linton for what Heathcliff does not have: money, position, ease: the visible elements of society. She thinks she can retain a double identity: the indestructible identity, the profound and the necessary, but also the contingent identity, the temporary the superficial and the pleasing. There is nothing unusual in this kind of betrayal, this characteristic error, and it can be interpreted from outside in a number of ways, given our alternative terms for the necessary and the permanent and for the kinds of denial, of detachment, which can then be described. But the action is specific. She takes Heathcliff for granted and she marries Linton, and the real dislocation —the disruption, the savagery, the storm—then inevitably follows. So great a breach is made in all necessary relationships that only in another generation, and then through time, is any effective fabric restored. But just because it was necessary the affirmative persists; indeed it goes beyond life, because it is in the life of another and in the shared reality of a place. Denied where it ought to have existed, it persists in an experienced transcendence: in what others see. Heathcliff, near the end, is still trying to live where the reality had been, but now in a terrible isolation because of the denial:

> In every cloud, in every tree—filling the air and night, and caught by glimpses in every object by day—I am surrounded with her image. The most ordinary faces of men and women—my own features—mock me with a resemblance. The entire world is a dreadful collection of memoranda that she did exist, and that I have lost her.

'Image', 'resemblance': that is the displacement, the mourned loss. What he feels is so ordinary that we need no special terms for it. It is that finding of reality in the being of another which is the necessary human identity: the identity of the human beyond the creature; the identity of relationship out of which all life comes. Deprived of this reality there is indeed only image and resemblance, and it is exactly right that even physical life then stops or must be willed:

> I have to remind myself to breathe—almost to remind my heart to beat.

Between the given and the willed, between the necessary and that plausible world which can appear to be separable, the action drives to its conclusion. A necessary experience of what it is to be human—of that life-desire, that relationship which is given—is frustrated, displaced, lost in those specific difficulties; but is then in a profoundly convincing way—just because it is necessary—echoed, reflected back, from where it now exists only in spirit: the image of the necessary, seen moving beyond that composed, that rearranged life; the reality of need, of the human need, haunting, appearing to, a limited scaled-down world.

When I say that *Wuthering Heights* is quite central to its time I don't mean its documentary element or what can be called its symbolism; the experience is so direct it doesn't have to be translated. It is the positive experience which has elsewhere been given a negative translation—a negative term—as alienation, and the process beyond that catchword is undoubtedly real. And because this is so, the organising experience of the novel is a more than personal desire, a more than personal longing. Indeed the intensity of persons has to be seen being displaced and then qualified, observed, interpreted; there and yet seen at a distance, seen in other modes; convincing and yet in necessary opposition with other persuasive versions of reality. And this is its critical difference from the ordinarily related fiction of intense and personal feeling.

Jane Eyre, for example, is in the world of *Wuthering Heights*, much more than we now usually admit. It is a structured presentation of some of the same urgent themes, with one critical difference: that its organising principle, its specific gravity, is quite directly personal. And this is of course much more than technique, though in that it shows clearly enough. *Jane Eyre* is first-person in a quite radical way where *Wuthering Heights* is multipersonal: an effect of experience before ever it is a method. The connecting power of Charlotte Brontë's fiction is in just this first-person capacity to compose an intimate relationship with the reader: from the easy friendly beginning—'I was glad of it, I never liked long walks'—to the final and secret sharing—'I kept these things then, and pondered them in my heart': things the reader knows but the others—the other characters, the outside world—do not.

'Reader, I married him'. But that address to the reader, that capital public address, is a late pulling-away as the story fades into retrospect, into the given account. While the experience lasts, the 'I' of the novel and the subjective position—the only available position—of the reader are on a much closer bearing. What matters throughout is this private confidence, this mode of confession: the account given as if in a private letter, in private talk; the account given to a journal, a private journal, and then the act of writing includes—as it were involuntarily, yet it is very deliberate and conscious art—the awareness of the friend, the close one, the unknown but in this way intimate reader: the reader *as* the writer, while the urgent voice lasts.

Given the action of *Jane Eyre*, which is in every sense dramatic, there is a pull, all the same, between action and consciousness: a tension and a power which relate it to *Wuthering Heights*. To see the full difference between the mode of *Wuthering Heights* and this persuasive personal mode of Charlotte Brontë's main fiction, we need to turn to *Villette*. Multipersonal and varied in consciousness: these decisive elements of *Wuthering Heights* have to do, I suggested, with *relationship*, with intense relationship and with its experienced alternatives. And then of course you can say that the directing impulse of all Charlotte's novels is also relationship: a desired relationship, actually more overtly desired and more apparently achieved in *Jane Eyre* or in *Villette* than at all in *Wuthering Heights*. The desire, I mean, gets through; the relationships seem to arrange themselves. But what I'm trying to say is that it *isn't* the same desire, the same kind of desire. This is very difficult because the word, the feeling, bears strongly both ways. But I've tried to distinguish between desire *for* another and desire *in* another: that distinction that is made, very closely made, in *Wuthering Heights* itself. Desire *for* another can be very intense and of course it is subject to all the accidents of the world: death, loss, disturbance, misunderstanding—those are continually important; but also those harder experiences—he is tied to another, involved with another; convention, law, property stand between; or still harder again—and it is not uncommon—the desire for another which is not returned, not responded to; yet the desire *for* is still intensely, painfully there. But desire *in* another: I don't say it's better, that doesn't arise, since it happens too deep, too early, for that kind of comment. I say only it's different because it's a relationship: I mean an achieved relationship, before anything else. A necessary relationship, in which a self, a world, is at once found and confirmed; and which of course—it's always happening, it's how the violence is done—can be broken, disastrously broken. And this is different, radically different, from the failure to find another, the failure to find a desired object, or the loss of a possession or what is desired to be possessed. These failures and losses are so breaking that we can easily run them together, but the essential process is always different; it is a question of how far, how necessarily, the life-connections are made.

Shall I yet see him before he goes? Will he bear me in mind? Does he purpose to come? Will this day—will the next hour bring him? or must I again assay that corroding pain of long attent—that rude agony of rupture at the close, that mute, mortal wrench, which, in at once uprooting hope and doubt, shakes life, while the hand that does the violence cannot be caressed to pity because absence interposes her barrier?

In passages like this from *Villette* Charlotte seizes a kind of experience—of frustration and waiting—which connects very closely with what I called the secret sharing: not the public process, though it can be generalised towards that—'that mute, mortal wrench which shakes life'—but the particular immediate experience. And this is indeed her strength. The prose is very different from anything in *Wuthering Heights* because the essential composition—the structure of the narrative—is quite other: is not multipersonal and varied, qualified and obscured in time, but subjective single and immediate:

What should I do; oh! *what* should I do; when all my life's hope was thus torn by the roots out of my outraged heart?

That is the exact movement: the recreated question to one-self that is specifically the question, the involving question, to the reader, the sharer; and then the rhetorical extension that tries to name the common emotion:

The hopes which are dear to youth, which bear it up and lead it on, I knew not and dared not know. If they knocked at my heart sometimes, an inhospitable bar to admission must be inwardly drawn. When they turned away thus rejected, tears sad enough sometimes flowed; but it could not be helped; I dared not give such guests lodging. So mortally did I fear the sin and weakness of presumption. Religious reader, you will preach to me a long sermon about what I have just written, and so will you, moralist; and you, stern sage: you, stoic, will frown; you cynic, sneer; you, epicure, laugh. Well each and all, take it your own way. I accept the sermon, frown, sneer, and laugh; perhaps you are all right: and perhaps, circumstanced like me, you would have been, like me, wrong.

I repeat, this is conscious art. The actual reader, feeling these other responses forming, is distanced, named; or to put it another way, those observing questioning criticising responses are distanced, so that the effective relation with the reader—and this is the only reader really in mind—can come powerfully through: 'circumstanced like me, you would have been . . .' and the 'perhaps' falls back into a forgotten distance; 'you would have been, like me'. 'Wrong?' But that doesn't arise, in the terms of the moralist or the sage. This is 'wrong' inside confession, inside intimate confession: a fault, if at all, within a wholly revealed, wholly accepted experience.

Seen in this early example, there is remarkable skill in the process of sympathy. The questions I quoted—'*What* should I do; oh! *what* should I do?—are present and suspended, with almost a pause for response, before the narrative moves, including many possibilities, to what I *should* have done, I know not, when a little child—the least child in the school—broke with its simplicity and unconsciousness into the raging yet silent centre of that inward conflict.

'The raging yet silent centre': this is what, in *Villette*, is heard. It is lonely unexpressed feeling, that has now found a voice. As in waiting desperately for a letter; finding somewhere quiet to read it, through all the noise of the classes:

'Will it be long—will it be short?' . . . It was long.
'Will it be cool—will it be kind?' It was kind.

The process is instantaneous, with no author ahead of it; and like the letter itself is meant for reading alone, somewhere quiet, where the relation, the sharing, is direct. I've noticed again and again—you've all probably noticed—how difficult it is reading *Villette* out, reading it out in public. For that isn't its world.

The poor English teacher in the frosty garret, reading by a dim candle guttering in the wintry air. . . . To my longing and famished thought . . .

It's that kind of closeness, that kind of recognition: like the mark in the margin of the book in the library—the secret sharing, the assent. And it's easy to destroy; dangerously easy; just as it's easy not to feel what went into that mark, that sharing, that silent recognition and reference.

I only wanted to define it and to show its difference from *Wuthering Heights*, where the light falls from so many directions, in so many accents, on an intensity that is worked, open and in that sense public: an intensity of stated relationship which is examined and lasts, persists, through the intricacies of observation and of time.

And I'd then say, finally, that Charlotte stands very obviously at the head of a tradition, in a way that her sister does not; and I think that is history, a significant history, when we come to reflect. For the method of *Villette* is what I called once, coldly, the fiction of special pleading. I mean that fiction in which the only major emotion, and then the relation with the reader, is that exact stress, that first-person stress: 'circumstanced like me'. The stress is this really: the world will judge me in certain ways if it sees what I do, but if it knew how I felt it would see me quite differently. And then the particular weakness of this form has become very obvious. Its persons outside this shaping longing demanding consciousness have reality only as they contribute to the landscape, the emotional landscape, of the special, the pleading, the recommending character. That is all we know of them, all we really know of her, and some extraordinary things have been done in its name: use of others, abuse of others; a breakdown of discourse—and with discourse so much else, so many other needs and realities—as the all-including voice, the voice pleading for this experience, for understanding of it, for the exclusion of alternatives—alternative voices, alternative viewpoints—comes through and creates its own world. I think that makes us now look back at *Villette* with a certain awe, a certain wariness. Certainly *Wuthering Heights* beside it is fresh and open air. But the power is there, the original power: the immediate personal and creative form: the inclusive sharing of what had been an unspoken voice, as opposed to that other extending, dislocating, affirming world.

III

George Eliot

G EORGE ELIOT once said that Charlotte Brontë's
 Villette was 'a still more wonderful book than *Jane Eyre*.
There is something almost preternatural in its power.' This is
not an admiration that fits our usual reading of the development
of the novel in England, but it is important and significant. To
pass from Lucy Snowe to Maggie Tulliver is to be in no doubt
about the family resemblance in the loneliness and frustration
of the isolated girl. And what is 'almost preternatural' is the
intense and overwhelming confession and working of this
private, as it were secret, emotion.

> Maggie drew a long breath and pushed her heavy hair back, as if
> to see a sudden vision more clearly.

Yet this sense of 'vision', in intense and isolated feeling, is connected profoundly with the need to understand realistically an
everyday world.

> She wanted some explanation of this hard, real life.

And this is no paradox. It is the emergence in the novel of that
structure of feeling of the greatest Romantic poetry: at once a
commitment to a personal vision and a passionate concern with
the social experiences of ordinary life. One of the key passages
in *Mill on the Floss* is in Chapter 3 of Book 4, where Maggie

> with her girl's face and unnoted sorrows, found an effort and a
> hope that helped her through years of loneliness, making out a
> faith for herself without the aid of established authorities and
> appointed guides.

She is reading, again characteristically, an author from the medieval past, Thomas à Kempis,

> the chronicle of a solitary, hidden anguish, struggle, trust, triumph.

The run of the feeling seems simple, but then as part of the sequence, for all its alteration of tone, comes a paragraph which begins:

> In writing the history of unfashionable families, one is apt to fall into a tone of emphasis which is very far from being the tone of good society.

What is connected suddenly here (by no 'established authorities' or 'appointed guides') is the intensity of lonely feeling and the hardness of ordinary life: a connection which we can best describe, in a significantly double sense, in a phrase she goes on to use—the emphasis of *want*. George Eliot's early work, directly connected in that way not only to the Brontës but to the strongest parts of the Romantic tradition, moves within this emphasis and connection. What we must then examine is the relation—the very difficult relation—in George Eliot's development, between the intense feeling which is so often in practice separating and isolating, and the practical extension in observation and sympathy of the ordinary community of the novel.

Is the connection of these experiences, we might ask first, only historical: only the coincidence, in an actual adolescence and now in memory, of intense lonely feeling and a practical sharing of ordinary working life? Certainly the internal relation is simpler when the whole structure is retrospective. This has an obvious relevance to George Eliot's practice of setting most of her novels back in time. But the more critical question is about the kind of sharing of ordinary life that is actually achieved. This bears directly on a problem which seems to me to be central in the subsequent development of the English novel: the real relations, in feeling and in form, between *edu-cated* and *customary* life and thought.

We can take a familiar example. It is often said of the Poysers in *Adam Bede* or of the Gleggs and the Dodsons in *Mill on the Floss* that they are marvellously (the alternative adverbs are warmly, richly, charmingly) done. But what this seems to me to point to is a recurring problem in the social consciousness of the writer. George Eliot's connections with the farmers and craftsmen—her connections as Mary Ann Evans—can be heard again and again in their language. Characteristically she presents them mainly through speech. But while they are present, audibly, as a community, they have only to emerge in significant action—that is to say in an action other than the generalising background of the novel—to change in quality. What Adam or Dinah or Hetty say when they are acting as individuals is not particularly convincing. Thus the farmers and craftsmen can be included as 'country people' but much less significantly as the active bearers of personal experience. When Adam and Dinah and Hetty talk in what is supposed to be personal crisis— or later in a more glaring case when Felix Holt talks—we are shifted to the level of generalised attitudes or of declamation. Another way of putting this would be to say that though George Eliot restored the real inhabitants of rural England to their places in what had been a socially selective landscape, she does not get much further than restoring them *as a landscape*. They begin to talk as it were collectively; as what middle-class critics still from a distance call a chorus, a 'ballad-element'; as 'characters' that is to say who—the critical term is exact, though not in the way it is usually meant—are 'done'. For as themselves they are still only socially present and can emerge into a higher consciousness only through externally formulated attitudes and ideas.

I would not make this point bitterly, for the difficulty is acute.

It is a contradiction in the form of the novel as George Eliot received and developed it. We would not willingly lose the Poysers the Gleggs and the Dodsons, but it is significant that we can talk of them in this way in the plural, while the emotional direction of the novels is more and more towards separated individuals.

This is a real history: indeed one of the clearest examples of literature enacting a history which is not otherwise, in any important way, articulated or recorded. It is very complicated once we take its full weight. There is the intense feeling of the isolated individual: isolated in the first instance by the structure of this feeling, because while the personal life is experienced the social life is mainly observed. Yet the more serious the observation, in a community that is taken as given—as there by the facts of birth and place—the more insistent the emphasis, the emphasis of want. And the way in which this very conflict between isolation and sympathy emerges is a matter of ideas: of consciousness, social consciousness, as a personal need—

she wanted some explanation of this hard real life.

We have already observed two positions: the intensity of isolated need and desire; the inherited sympathy of general observation. We must now add a third: the analytic consciousness, that ordinary product of individual and social development, which comes in to enlighten and to qualify but above all to mediate the isolated desire and the general observation. George Eliot's genius is that she is fully exposed—that she exposes herself—over this whole range. She has precedents for each faculty in the previous development of the novel, but for the combination of these faculties—the necessary combination for the next and difficult creative stage—she has no precedents. She has to create a new form on her own, under the pressures of what are not merely different but conflicting actions and

78

methods. In the very texture of her writing, in the basic construction of her novels, she has to resolve a conflict of grammars: a conflict of 'I' and 'we' and 'they', and then of the impersonal constructions that in a way inevitably come to substitute for each.

That is the necessary contrast with Dickens: the contrast that has to be at the centre of any serious analysis of nineteenth-century English writing. The strength of Dickens's position is that he could base himself on an existing social formation: on an urban popular culture which in its amalgam of strengths and weaknesses had an available, a directly communicating, grammar. But George Eliot's social formation was at best only emerging: a guarantee of connection to our own world in which each of its separate processes has gone further and deeper, but in her own world conflicting, pulling different ways, setting conscious problems in each story, almost each sentence, she must write. She extends the community of the novel, as we have already seen. She develops the idiom of individual moral analysis into a world in which morality is both individual and social: the quality of a way of life in the qualities of persons. She faces the new problems of intense vision within, uneasily within, a hard real life.

But whereas the idiom of the novelist in Jane Austen was quite closely connected with the idiom of the characters, in George Eliot a disconnection is the most evident fact, and the novelist herself is very acutely aware of this. Or compare the idiom of Charlotte Brontë, sustaining intense feeling but cutting its connections with an intrusive or controlling consciousness; driving the single feeling through, but at the expense of any extended, any placing observation. George Eliot, by contrast, forces the feeling and the consciousness together, but of course uneasily. There is then a new kind of break in the texture of the novel: between the narrative idiom of the novelist and the recorded language of her characters; between the analytic idiom and the overwhelming emphasis of emotion.

Most novelists develop, but George Eliot, I would say, had almost to create a new form, each time, if she was to go on with this whole and uneasy experience. If in looking at this process we see, as we must, certain radical failures, we have to refer them in the end to this underlying and transforming growth and extension: a creative and experimental process which took all her great powers.

This is the right way, I think, to see the relation in her work between the consciousness of the writer and the knowable community: that relation which I see as the key to this history. Let us complete that paragraph, in *Mill on the Floss*, which we referred to earlier.

In writing the history of unfashionable families, one is apt to fall into a tone of emphasis which is very far from being the tone of good society, where principles and beliefs are not only of an extremely moderate kind, but are always presupposed, no subjects being eligible but such as can be touched with a light and graceful irony. But then, good society has its claret and its velvet carpets, its dinner-engagements six weeks deep, its opera and its fairy ballrooms; rides off its *ennui* on thoroughbred horses, lounges at the club, has to keep clear of crinoline vortices, gets its science done by Faraday, and its religion by the superior clergy who are to be met in the best houses: how should it have time or need for belief and emphasis? But good society, floated on gossamer wings of light irony, is of very expensive production; requiring nothing less than a wide and arduous natural life condensed in unfragrant, deafening factories, cramping itself in mines, sweating at furnaces, grinding, hammering, weaving under more or less oppression of carbonic acid—or else, spread over sheep-walks, and scattered in lonely houses and huts on the clayey or chalky corn-lands, where the rainy days look dreary. This wide national life is based entirely on emphasis—the emphasis of want, which urges it into all the activities necessary for the maintenance of good society and light irony. . . .

What we have to say, I think, about this memorable argument
is that it is at once the common problem and the individual
response. The emphasis of want is undoubtedly central in
George Eliot, and she sees work here as it is, without any sentimental contrast between the town and the village labourer.
Emphasis as a class feeling: this is what she acknowledges and
accepts. But then it has to be noticed that she writes of it with
her own brand of irony; she is defensive and self-conscious in
the very demonstration of emphasis, so that in this structure of
communication the very poor become the 'unfashionable'. Her
central seriousness and yet her acute consciousness of other and
often congenial tones is at once a paradox of language and of
community. We find this again in two characteristic passages
in *Adam Bede*:

> Paint us an angel, if you can, with a flowing violet robe, and a
> face paled by the celestial light; paint us yet oftener a Madonna,
> turning her mild face upward and opening her arms to welcome
> the divine glory; but do not impose on us any aesthetic rules which
> shall banish from the region of Art those old women scraping
> carrots with their work-worn hands, those heavy clowns taking
> holiday in a dingy pot-house, those rounded backs and stupid
> weather-beaten faces that have bent over the spade and done the
> rough work of the world— those homes with their tin pans, their
> brown pitchers, their rough curs, and their clusters of onions. In
> this world there are so many of these common coarse people, who
> have no picturesque sentimental wretchedness. It is so needful we
> should remember their existence. . . .
>
> I am not ashamed of commemorating old Kester: you and I are
> indebted to the hard hands of such men—hands that have long
> ago mingled with the soil they tilled so faithfully, thriftily making
> the best they could of the earth's fruits, and receiving the smallest
> share as their own wages.

The declaration is again serious and emphatic, but who is being
spoken to in the anxious plea: 'do not impose on us any aesthetic
rules which shall banish . . .'? Who made the compact of 'you

and I' who must be shown as indebted? Who, finally, provoked the consciousness which requires the acknowledgement 'I am not ashamed', and its associated language of 'clowns' and 'stupid weather-beaten faces', mixing as it so strangely does with the warmth of memory of the kitchens and with the truth about wages, the firm rejection of 'picturesque sentimental wretchedness'.

In passages like these and in the novels from which they are taken, George Eliot has extended the real social range of the novel—its knowable community—and yet is more self-conscious than any of her predecessors; more uneasily placating and appealing to what seems a dominant image of a particular kind of reader. The knowable community is this common life, which she is pleased to record with a necessary emphasis. But the known community, creatively known, is something else again—an uneasy contract, in language, with another interest and another sensibility.

What is true of language is true of action. George Eliot extends the plots of her novels to include the farmers and the craftsmen, and also the disinherited. But just as she finds it difficult to individuate working people—falling back on a choral mode, a generalising description, or an endowment with her own awkwardly translated consciousness—so she finds it difficult to conceive whole actions which spring from the substance of these lives, and which can be worked through in direct and controlling relation to who and what they are. *Adam Bede* is the nearest to this, but it is overridden, finally, by an external interest. Hetty is a subject till that last moment on the road, before she abandons her baby. From that point on she is an object: of confession and conversion, of *attitudes* towards suffering. This is the essential difference from Hardy's *Tess of the D'Urbervilles* which has the strength to keep to the subject to the end. Adam Bede and Dinah Morris—as one might say

the dignity of self-respecting labour and religious enthusiasm—
are more important in the end. Even the changed repentant
Arthur is more important than the girl whom the novelist
abandons, in a moral action more decisive than Hetty's own
confused and desperate leaving of her child.

Yet still the history is active: the finding of continuity in the
stress of learned feelings. *The Mill on the Floss* is the crisis of
this determining history. It is an action from within the emphasis of want: in the guarded unattractive rituals of survival of the
small farmers, the Dodsons; in the rash independence of Tulliver, broken by the complications of law and economic pressure
that he does not understand. But in neither of those ways can
any fulness of life be achieved, and there is no way through
where the novelist's feelings really go; only the weak unwilled
temporary escape of the trip on the river: the fantasy of com-
fort. What is then made to happen, because it is all that can
happen, is a return to childhood and the river; a return, releas-
ing feeling, to a transcending death. From the common history,
which had been primary, the curve of feeling moves to a re-
nunciation, an isolation; to the exposed and separated individual in whom the only action of value is located. And then
what can be in these early novels an active desperate isolation
becomes in her later work a sad though still intense resignation.

In the later novels, for all their evidence of growing maturity
and control, the actions become more external to that common
world in which the emphasis of want was decisive. As if over-
come by the dead weight of the interests of a separated and
propertied class—the supposed class of her readers, the educated
class to which she now directly relates—the plots of the later
works are in a different world. *Felix Holt*, a portrait of radicalism, is made to turn on of all things the inheritance of an
estate. This is a surrender to that typical interest which preoccupied the nineteenth-century middle-class imagination. Of

course Esther rejects the inheritance in the end. That is part of the real history. George Eliot's moral emphasis is too genuinely of an improving kind, of a self-making and self-made life, to permit Esther to accept the inheritance and find the fashionable way out. The corruption of that inheriting world, in which the price of security is intrigue and self-betrayal, is powerfully shown in Mrs Transome and in Jermyn. But the emphasis of want is now specialised to Felix Holt: to the exposed, separated, potentially mobile individual. It is part of a crucial history in the development of the novel, in which the knowable community —the extended and emphatic world of an actual rural and then industrial England—comes to be known primarily as a problem of relationship: of how the separated individual, with a divided consciousness of belonging and not belonging, makes his own moral history.

This is the source of the disturbance, the unease, the divided construction of the later George Eliot novels (the exception for reasons we shall see is *Middlemarch*). We have only to compare George Eliot with her contemporary Anthony Trollope to see the significance of this disturbance. Trollope in his Barsetshire novels is at ease with schemes of inheritance, with the inter-action of classes and interests, with the lucky discovery and the successful propertied marriage. For his essential interest is all in how it happens, how it is done. An even, easy narrative tone, with a minimum both of analysis and of individual disturbance, can achieve all that is asked of it: a recorded observation, an explanation, at that level of social mechanics. To read *Doctor Thorne* beside *Felix Holt* is not only to find ease in Trollope, where there is disturbance in George Eliot; to find a level of interest corresponding with the plot instead of interests struggling to break free of a dutifully sustained and external compli-cation; to find the conventional happy ending where property and happiness can coexist and be celebrated, rather than an awkward stubborn unappeased resignation. It is also, quite evidently, to see the source of these differences in a real social history. And I think we have to remember this when we are asked by several kinds of critic to abstract 'construction', 'organisation', 'thematic unity', 'unity of tone' and even 'good writing' and judge novels by those canons. On these abstract criteria—and especially those of unity—we should have to find Trollope a better novelist than George Eliot. What we have to emphasise, on the contrary, is the creative disturbance which is exactly George Eliot's importance: the disturbance we shall see also in Hardy. That is where the life is, in that disturbed and unprecedented time. And those who responded most deeply, who saw most, had no unified form, no unity of tone and language, no controlling conventions, that really answered their purposes. Their novels are the records of struggle and difficulty, as was the life they wrote about.

Take for comparison the beginning of Trollope's *Doctor Thorne*. He can announce with characteristic confidence the state of his rural England:

> Its green pastures, its waving wheat, its deep and shady and—let us add—dirty lanes, its paths and stiles, its tawny-coloured, well-built rural churches, its avenues of beeches, and frequent Tudor mansions, its constant county hunt, its social graces, and the air of clanship which pervades it, has made it to its own inhabitants a favoured land of Goshen. It is purely agricultural: agricultural in its produce, agricultural in its poor, and agricultural in its pleasures.

Here the extent of realism is the mannered concession that the lanes are dirty. For the rest what is seen is a social structure with pastoral trimmings. The agricultural poor are placed, easily, between the produce and the pleasures. And while this easy relationship holds, there is no moral problem of any consequence to disturb the smooth and recommending construction.

England is not yet a commercial country in the sense in which that epithet is used for her; and let us hope that she will not soon become so. She might surely as well be called feudal England, or chivalrous England. If in western civilised Europe there does exist a nation among whom there are high signors, and with whom the owners of the land are the true aristocracy, the aristocracy that is trusted as being best and fitted to rule, that nation is the English.

As a description of mid-nineteenth century England, this is ludicrous. But as a way of seeing it without extended question it is perfect. It takes the values for granted and can then study, with a persistent accuracy, the internal difficulties of the class, and especially the problem of the relation between the inheriting landed families and the connected and rising cadet and professional people. Trollope shares an interest in getting into that class, which is what the inheritance plot had always mainly served, and he can describe its processes without difficulty or illusion (once the basic illusion of describing the landowners as an aristocracy has been accepted).

George Eliot, by contrast, questioning in a profoundly moral way the real and assumed relations between property and human quality, accepts the emphasis of inheritance as the central action and then has to make it external, contradictory and finally irrelevant, as her real interest transfers to the separated exposed individual, who becomes sadly resigned, or must go away. What happens to the Transomes' land, in *Felix Holt*, or to Grandcourt's, in *Daniel Deronda*, is no longer decisive; yet around the complications of that kind of interest a substantial part of each novel has been built. In this sense George Eliot's novels are transitional between that form which could end in a series of settlements, in which the social and economic solutions and the personal achievements were in a single dimension, and that new form which extending and complicating and then finally collapsing this dimension ends with a single person going away on his own, having achieved his moral growth by distancing or by extrication. It is a divided consciousness of belonging and not belonging. The social solutions—the common solutions—are still taken seriously up to the last point of personal crisis, and then what is achieved as a personal moral development has to express itself as some kind of physical or spiritual renewal; an emigration, at once resigned and hopeful, from what had originally been offered as a decisive social world.

It is worth considering this pattern in relation to *Middlemarch* which I have already suggested is in important ways an exception in her mature work. George Eliot became so conscious of history as a social and as a moral process that the problem of most of her work after *Mill on the Floss* is the discovery of an action which is capable of expressing it in its real connections. In the early novels the essential connections are *given*; one wants to say 'in retrospect' but that isn't at all how it feels. It isn't *looking* back, it's more like taking a whole experience straight out of the past, an experience already complete in itself, on which it is true the author makes marginal comments, but then the point is that the margin—the later consciousness—is visible and external.

Looking back in any full sense begins in *The Mill on the Floss* but is only determining in the novels after *Romola*—an experiment indeed which confirms the transition. The organisation of *Felix Holt* and then again of *Daniel Deronda* is in effect an organisation around an idea: of radicalism, in *Felix Holt*; of something very new and difficult to name—not just Zionism nor only internationalism, but in that area of the crossing of frontiers, the transcendence of customary communities, not by a loss of loyalties but by a discovery of new loyalties to other peoples, other kinds of life, and through them to an idea of connecting humanity—in *Daniel Deronda*. Whereas in the earlier novels value is in the past, as a general condition—an intrinsically valuing society, the common condition of a knowable community—in the later work value has to be created, just because of the new and emphatic consciousness of historical *process* (a very different matter from a simple awareness, as between past and present, of historical *change*). And then the difficulty of *Felix Holt*, and the more familiar difficulty of *Daniel Deronda*, lies in the capacity of this idea to generate connected life. For what is in fact perceived, against the run of the idea, is an experience of disconnection, even radical dislocation, by which when the connections of plot are revealed the effect is the opposite to that of Dickens: is not the sense of a reconciling common humanity, the kind of miracle Dickens enacts, but of complicated and perhaps intractable difficulty—not the network but the web.

I drew attention, in *Culture and Society*, to George Eliot's use of these metaphors—'network' and 'web', 'a tangled business'—to describe actual social relations. But I think we have to go on to distinguish the different bearings of this complicated image. The network, we might say, connects; the web, the tangle, disturbs and obscures. To discover a network, to feel human connection in what is essentially a knowable community, is to assert (I mean assert creatively, produce as an experience) a particular social value: a necessary interdependence. But to discover a web or a tangle is to see human relationships as not only involving but compromising, limiting, mutually frustrating. And this is of course a radically different consciousness: what is still called a modern consciousness; in fact the first phase of a post-liberal world: a period between cultures, in which the old confidence of individual liberation has gone and the new commitment to social liberation has not yet been made. George Eliot moves more powerfully than any of our novelists in that profoundly difficult transitional world. The ideas of *Felix Holt* and of *Daniel Deronda* are positive moves to surpass it; but the

radicalism of the first ends by confirming the sense of a deadlock; and the faith of the second is an effective emigration—not
the functional emigration of earlier nineteenth-century novels,
as in Elizabeth Gaskell or Kingsley, the guiding of loved
characters to a simpler and happier land, but a spiritual emigration, a deeply felt, deeply desired transcendence.

Middlemarch stands between these attempts but its process is
different. There is no overt dislocation, no pull inside the novel
towards separable worlds across which accidental connections
are made by the mechanics of plot. What is found in *Middlemarch* is a knowable community, but knowable in a new sense.
Socially it is in some ways contracted. The country labourers
talking of the railway are a brief chorus: 'this is the big folks's
world'. The town craftsmen are also a chorus, characteristically
heard in the pubs: 'Mr Crabbe the glazier' and other representative happy families, talking sharply but instrumentally about
their social superiors, the main characters of the novel.

But then within this real circle Middlemarch is a remarkably
integrated society. It is a provincial town with its necklace
villages, or looked at the other way, the main way of the novel,
it is a system of parishes with this new and growing organism
somewhat ambiguously at its centre; 'municipal town and rural
parish gradually made fresh threads of connexion', in a phase
just preceding the full effects of industrialism. Middlemarch,
like Coventry in the 1820s and 1830s, is a town of small textile
manufacturers: braid-making, ribbon-making and dyeing; still
employing some handloom weavers and outworkers; with a
traditional county town and a new industrial town, Brassing,
not far away. Vincy the manufacturer and Bulstrode the banker
are there in the town, but the social consciousness begins and
ends in the landed society into which these new forces are
growing. It is Brooke, with his abstract ideas of reform, who
brings the main characters together, not without some protest

from Mrs Cadwallader; and the professional men—doctors and clergymen—moving about 'disregarding the Middlemarch discrimination of ranks' are also the 'threads of connexion'. George Eliot refers to the real processes within this sort of society—the steady rise and fall of families—as 'those less marked vicissitudes which are constantly shifting the boundaries of social intercourse and begetting new consciousness of interdependence'. This is a changing but still knowable community, except that something else is happening: what she calls 'the double change of self and beholder'. That I believe is what is really new in the novel, because it affects, profoundly, the novelist's essential method.

Middlemarch in every way is less given than taken: taken, consciously, in 'the double change of self and beholder'. An older mode of awareness is still present in the Garths; I mean in the way George Eliot sees the Garths, as we see our own families—present, whole, simply there, before anything needs to be said about them. Mary Garth is not formally described, given analysing discriminating features, until some time after she has been effectively present. It is as we might stare and reflect, in some moment of adverted attention, at someone we already effectively know, simply know and are with. But the dominant consciousness is quite different: a signifying consciousness: not of the known or the knowable but of the to-be-known; in a sense, a decisive sense, the *objects* of consciousness. Dorothea has elements of Maggie Tulliver, but she is now at arm's length being looked at. Virtually all the other characters and indeed the society are looked at, examined, in this public way: 'the double change in self and beholder'.

It is a consciousness, a fictional method, that has been widely recommended. It is referred back to the cool 'impersonality' of Jane Austen; forward to the wrought observation of Henry James and thence to what is often called, in a sweeping indeed overbearing dimension, maturity. The difference from Jane Austen, the deciding difference, is that not only the characters but the way of life they compose come under this conscious examination. The difference from many later examples is also this: for it is a method that when abstracted is a cold placing, a critic's fiction. Indeed, more than that, it is a social mode in which the observer, the signifier, is not himself at stake but is refined into a fictional process, indeed into a fiction. At its lower levels, which have been very popular, it is the mode of an anxious society—an anxious class preoccupied with placing, grading, defining: the sharp enclosing phrases about others as they leave the room, and a kind of willing forgetfulness that it will happen to the phrasers as they also leave. It's the staple of a familiar— sometimes witty sometimes malicious—minor fiction, and of a whole world of small talk. As you'll have gathered, I don't really find it particularly mature, though when it bears down on you in a whole place—in a university for example—it has an apparent poise that takes some time to live through: a mode in which we are all signifiers, all critics and judges, and can somehow afford to be because life—given life, creating life—goes on where it is supposed to, elsewhere.

I've pushed it that far, from its much more substantial more affirmed existence in *Middlemarch*, as a way of registering a profound unease—an unease that of course goes along with respect—about the coldness, the picking, of those parts of the novel. I think it was inevitable. It is a dislocation, not of an overt kind but very deep and substantial: the dislocation in consciousness, 'the double change in self and beholder'. *Middlemarch* as a whole is a superb presentation, a superb analysis: that *is* its consciousness. As a way of seeing, it is so powerfully composed that it creates its own conditions, enacts and re-enacts its own kind of achievement. It has been so praised so often in just that sense that I don't need to add any other tributary adjectives. I want only to say that as a kind of consciousness it is really a portent: reminding us of that other meaning of 'known' and 'knowable', where the knower has become a separated process in himself: a profoundly serious but also profoundly accepted alienation.

'Anyone watching keenly the stealthy convergence of human lots': that phrase from *Middlemarch* defines the method exactly and defines the relationships, the substantial relationships, that are now knowable and known. It is the web in a new sense; the web we are watching from outside. The profound satisfaction this seems actually to give isn't anything I can argue against; it is an earlier choice of one life or another. All I'd add for emphasis (though it may emphasise only the shock, the inevitable shock of the breach of that convention) is that George Eliot can be seen as trying to pull free, trying to reach beyond that connecting, interlocking threaded consciousness. I believe she attempts this in Ladislaw, and it's very significant that we've had a parade of English critics disapproving of Ladislaw in very uniform ways. That he's unconvincing: that first ploy that is tried, but what is it, in a character, that 'convinces'?; it depends on general experience quite as much as on what is actually done with the fiction. Really, I suppose, that he's not 'one of us'; and that, listening, I'd grant. Indeed I think that's the point, and I'd add that some of these critics speaking with active distaste of Ladislaw sound remarkably like Mrs Cadwallader.

But it's more than old snobbery. It's what Ladislaw does. Lydgate fails; Casaubon fails; Brooke is inadequate; Cheetham is limited; Rosamund is trivial; Bulstrode is exposed. The Garths are stable; they last from an older world. And that pattern is clear, very clearly acceptable. In that older world there was stability and value; in the newer world, only complication, the web, a tangled business. The record is then of failure, frustration, resignation. And human fineness, human insight, is also that; sadly, wisely that: a stealthy convergence of human lots that has this valuable by-product, a wise settling insight.

And what can then be made of Ladislaw and of Dorothea marrying him? He's an offence, an obvious offence against that kind of settlement. Perhaps you've noticed how often critics refer to his hair; the tone is exactly one we've heard often recently about young men in the sixties; and in fact there's a connection. For Ladislaw is a free man in the way the others are not; a free mind with free emotions; a man who is wholly responsive. He isn't tied by property, which he can reject in a principled way. He's not of 'good birth' and doesn't try to depend on it. He has nothing on his side but his own feelings, his own actions, yet he understands art and learning better than Casaubon and reforms much better than Brooke. He makes friends with everyone he meets, including the 'unimportant' people; and he suffers from the will of both kinds of property, the inherited and the commercial. But since unlike Lydgate he can accept poverty, he is not frustrated, is not corrupted, does not become resigned. Coming from 'nowhere', belonging 'nowhere', he is able to move, to relate and so to grow in ways that the others are not. And it is to this, after all, that Dorothea responds.

'Unconvincing'. It is convenient, surely, to conclude that. For this is George Eliot thinking beyond, feeling beyond, the restrictions and the limitations she has so finely recorded; thinking into mobility not as dislocating but as liberating; with some anxiety, certainly—some registered qualified anxiety— but following a thread to the future, as she tried in *Daniel Deronda*; a single thread that has come loose from the web, but that she insists is there, running beyond Middlemarch as she herself ran beyond it: a responsiveness and a courage to live in new ways, under the weight, the defining weight, of a limited and frustrating world.

The main point, in the end, is still the defining consciousness: the method that predominates, the method that was learned. She is a great novelist in precisely that mode: a mode she achieved, literally made, out of profound disturbance and tension. And if the tension is there to the end—a different thread to the future in that superbly observed, superbly managed and limiting, defining world—that too is as it should be. She is giving her last strength, her deep warmth, to a hope, a possibility beyond what she had to record in a hardening clearly seen world.

IV

Thomas Hardy

IT is now conventional in critical accounts of the English novel to go on from George Eliot to Henry James. There is of course a real relation there, especially from parts of George Eliot's later novels—from the Transomes in *Felix Holt*, from Dorothea's relationships in *Middlemarch*, from Gwendolen and Grandcourt in *Daniel Deronda*. We shall need to follow that through.

But first I am interested in emphasising a more central English tradition: from George Eliot to Hardy and then on to Lawrence, which is a very clear and in my view decisive sequence. Some years ago a British Council critic described George Eliot, Hardy and Lawrence as 'our three great autodidacts', and as it happens his prejudice serves to indicate a very crucial fact. Why, we must ask, 'autodidact'? For all three of these writers were actively interested in learning and while they read a good deal for themselves had also a significant formal education. Their fathers were a bailiff a builder and a miner. George Eliot was at school till sixteen and left only because her mother died and she had to go home to look after her father, though she still took regular lessons there. Hardy was at Dorchester High School till the same age and then completed his professional training as an architect. Lawrence went into the sixth form at Nottingham High School and after a gap went on to Nottingham University College. It is not only that by their contemporary standards these levels of formal education are high. It is also that they are higher, absolutely, than those of four out of five people in mid-twentieth-century Britain. The flat patronage of 'autodidact' can then be related to only one fact: that none of the three was in the pattern of boarding-school and Oxbridge which in the late nineteenth century came to be regarded not simply as a kind of education but as education itself. To have missed that circuit was to have missed being 'educated' at all. In other words a 'standard' education was that received by one or two per cent of the population. All the rest were seen as 'uneducated' or else as 'autodidacts' (the later phrase was grammar-school-boy and will soon, no doubt, be comprehensive.) They were seen also, of course, as either comically ignorant or when they pretended to learning as awkward, overearnest, fanatical.

The effects of this on the English imagination have been deep. To many of us, now, George Eliot, Hardy and Lawrence are important because they connect directly with our own kind of upbringing and education. They belong to a cultural tradition much older and more central in this country than the comparatively modern and deliberately exclusive circuit of what are called the public schools. And the point is that they continue to connect in this way, into a later period in which some of us have gone to Oxford or Cambridge; to myself, for instance, who came from that kind of family to Cambridge and now teach here. For it is not the education, the developed intelligence, that is really in question. How many people, if it came to it, on the British Council or anywhere else, could survive a strictly intellectual comparison with George Eliot? It is a question of the relation between education—not the marks or degrees but the substance of a developed intelligence—and the actual lives of a continuing majority of our people: people who are not, by any formula, objects of record or study or concern, but who are specifically, literally, our own families. George Eliot is the first major novelist in whom this question is active. That is why we speak of her now with a connecting respect,

and with a hardness—a sort of family plainness—that we have
learned from our own and common experience.

It is also why we come to Hardy with interest and respect.
The more I read Hardy the surer I am that he is a major
novelist, but also that the problem of describing his work is
central to the problem of understanding the whole development of the English novel. It is good that so many people still
read him, and also that English students are reading him increasingly and with increasing respect. Yet some influential
critical accounts have tried to push him aside, and even some
of those who have praised him have done so in ways that reduce
him. Thus he can very easily be praised as what we now call a
regional novelist: the incomparable chronicler of his Wessex.
Or he can be taken as the last voice of an old rural civilisation.
The acknowledgement, even the warm tribute, comes with
the sense that the substance of his work is getting further and
further away from us: that he is not a man of our world but
the last representative of old rural England or of the peasantry.

Actually, the very complicated feelings and ideas in Hardy's
novels, including the complicated feelings and ideas about
country life and people, belong very much, I think, in a continuing world. He writes more consistently and more deeply
than any of our novelists about something that is still very close
to us wherever we may be living: something that can be put, in
abstraction, as the problem of the relation between customary
and educated life; between customary and educated feeling and
thought. This is the problem we already saw in George Eliot
and that we shall see again in Lawrence. It is the ground of their
significant connection.

Most of us, before we get any kind of literary education, get
to know and to value—also to feel the tensions of—a customary
life. We see and learn from the ways our families live and get
their living; a world of work and of place, and of beliefs so

deeply dissolved into everyday actions that we don't at first even know they are beliefs, subject to change and challenge. Our education, quite often, gives us a way of looking at that life which can see other values beyond it: as Jude saw them when he looked across the land to the towers of Christminster. Often we know in ourselves, very deeply, how much those educated values, those intellectual pursuits, are needed urgently where custom is stagnation or where old illusions are still repeated as timeless truths. We know especially how much they are needed to understand *change*—change in the heart of the places where we have lived and worked and grown up.

The ideas, the values, the educated methods are of course made available to us if we get to a place like Christminster: if we are let in as Jude was not. But with the offer, again and again, comes another idea: that the world of everyday work and of ordinary families is inferior, distant; that now we know this world of the mind we can have no respect—and of course no affection—for that other and still familiar world. If we retain an affection Christminster has a name for it: nostalgia. If we retain respect Christminster has another name: politics or the even more dreaded sociology.

But it is more than a matter of picking up terms and tones. It is what happens to us, really happens to us, as we try to mediate those contrasted worlds: as we stand with Jude but a Jude who has been let in; or as we go back to our own places, our own families, and know what is meant, in idea and in feeling, by the return of the native.

The Hardy country is of course Wessex: that is to say mainly Dorset and its neighbouring counties. But the real Hardy country, I feel more and more, is that border country so many of us have been living in: between custom and education, between work and ideas, between love of place and an experience of change. This has a special importance to a particular

generation, who have gone to the university from ordinary
families and have to discover, through a life, what that experience means. But it has also a much more general importance; for in Britain generally this is what has been happening:
a moving out from old ways and places and ideas and feelings;
a discovery in the new of certain unlooked-for problems, unexpected and very sharp crises, conflicts of desire and possibility.

In this characteristic world, rooted and mobile, familiar yet
newly conscious and self-conscious, the figure of Hardy stands
like a landmark. It is not from an old rural world or from a
remote region that Hardy now speaks to us; but from the heart
of a still active experience, of the familiar and the changing,
which we can know as an idea but which is important finally in
what seem the personal pressures—the making and failing of
relationships, the crises of physical and mental personality—
which Hardy as a novelist at once describes and enacts.

But of course we miss all this, or finding it we do not know
how to speak of it and value it, if we have picked up, here and
there, the tone of belittling Hardy.

I want to bring this into the open. Imagine if you will the
appearance and the character of the man who wrote this:

> When the ladies retired to the drawing-room I found myself
> sitting next to Thomas Hardy. I remember a little man with an
> earthy face. In his evening clothes, with his boiled shirt and high
> collar, he had still a strange look of the soil.

Not the appearance and the character of Thomas Hardy; but
of the man who could write that about him, that confidently,
that sure of his readers, in just those words.

It is of course Somerset Maugham, with one of his characteristic tales after dinner. It is a world, one may think, Hardy
should never have got near; never have let himself be exposed
to. But it is characteristic and important, all the way from that
dinner-table and that drawing-room to the 'look of the soil', in

that rural distance. All the way to the land, the work, that comes up in silver as vegetables, or to the labour that enters that company—that customary civilised company—with what is seen as an earthy face.

In fact I remember Maugham, remember his tone, when I read Henry James on

the good little Thomas Hardy

or F. R. Leavis saying that *Jude the Obscure* is impressive 'in its clumsy way'. For in several ways, some of them unexpected, we have arrived at that place where custom and education, one way of life and another, are in the most direct and interesting and I'd say necessary conflict.

The tone of social patronage, that is to say, supported by crude and direct suppositions about origin, connects interestingly with a tone of literary patronage and in ways meant to be damaging with a strong and directing supposition about the substance of Hardy's fiction. If he was a countryman, a peasant, a man with the look of the soil, then this is the point of view, the essential literary standpoint, of the novels. That is to say the fiction is not only about Wessex peasants, it is by one of them, who of course had managed to get a little (though hardly enough) education. Some discriminations of tone and fact have then to be made.

First, we had better drop 'peasant' altogether. Where Hardy lived and worked, as in most other parts of England, there were virtually no peasants, although 'peasantry' as a generic word for country people was still used by writers. The actual country people were landowners, tenant farmers, dealers, craftsmen and labourers, and that social structure—the actual material, in a social sense, of the novels—is radically different, in its variety, its shading, and many of its basic human attitudes from the structure of a peasantry. Secondly, Hardy is none of these people. Outside his writing he was one of the many professional men who worked within this structure, often with uncertainty about where they really belonged in it. A slow gradation of classes is characteristic of capitalism anywhere, and of rural capitalism very clearly. Hardy's father was a builder who employed six or seven workmen. Hardy did not like to hear their house referred to as a cottage, because he was aware of this employing situation. The house is indeed quite small but there is a little window at the back through which the men were paid, and the cottages down the lane are certainly smaller. At the same time, on his walk to school, he would see the mansion of Kingston Maurward (now happily an agricultural college) on which his father did some of the estate work, and this showed a sudden difference of degree which made the other distinction comparatively small though still not unimportant. In becoming an architect and a friend of the family of a vicar (the kind of family, also, from which his wife came) Hardy moved to a different point in the social structure, with connections to the educated but not the owning class, and yet also with connections through his family to that shifting body of small employers, dealers, craftsmen and cottagers who were themselves never wholly distinct, in family, from the labourers. Within his writing his position is similar. He is neither owner nor tenant, dealer nor labourer, but an observer and chronicler, often again with uncertainty about his actual relation. Moreover he was not writing for them, but about them, to a mainly metropolitan and unconnected literary public. The effect of these two points is to return attention to where it properly belongs, which is Hardy's attempt to describe and value a way of life with which he was closely yet uncertainly connected, and the literary methods which follow from the nature of this attempt. As so often when the current social stereotypes are removed the critical problem becomes clear in a new way.

It is the critical problem of so much of English fiction, since the actual yet incomplete and ambiguous social mobility of the nineteenth century. And it is a question of substance as much as of method. It is common to reduce Hardy's fiction to the impact of an urban alien on the 'timeless pattern' of English rural life. Yet though this is sometimes there the more common pattern is the relation between the changing nature of country living, determined as much by its own pressures as by pressures from 'outside', and one or more characters who have become in some degree separated from it yet who remain by some tie of family inescapably involved. It is here that the social values are dramatised in a very complex way and it is here that most of the problems of Hardy's actual writing seem to arise.

One small and one larger point may illustrate this argument, in a preliminary way. Nearly everyone seems to treat Tess as simply the passionate peasant girl seduced from outside, and it is then surprising to read quite early in the novel one of the clearest statements of what has become a classical experience of mobility:

> Mrs. Durbeyfield habitually spoke the dialect; her daughter, who had passed the Sixth Standard in the National School under a London-trained mistress, spoke two languages: the dialect at home, more or less; ordinary English abroad and to persons of quality.

Grace in *The Woodlanders*, Clym in *The Return of the Native* represent this experience more completely, but it is in any case a continuing theme, at a level much more important than the trivialities of accent. And when we see this we need not be tempted, as so often and so significantly in recent criticism, to detach *Jude the Obscure* as a quite separate kind of novel.

A more remarkable example of what this kind of separation means and involves is a description of Clym in *The Return of the*

Native which belongs in a quite central way to the argument I traced in *Culture and Society*:

> Yeobright loved his kind. He had a conviction that the want of most men was knowledge of a sort which brings wisdom rather than affluence. He wished to raise the class at the expense of individuals rather than individuals at the expense of the class. What was more, he was ready at once to be the first unit sacrificed.

The idea of sacrifice relates in the whole action to the familiar theme of a vocation thwarted or damaged by a mistaken marriage, and we shall have to look again at this characteristic Hardy deadlock. But it relates also to the general action of change which is a persistent social theme. As in all major realist fiction the quality and destiny of persons and the quality and destiny of a whole way of life are seen in the same dimension and not as separable issues. It is Hardy the observer who sets this context for personal failure:

> In passing from the bucolic to the intellectual life the intermediate stages are usually two at least, frequently many more; and one of these stages is sure to be worldly advance. We can hardly imagine bucolic placidity quickening to intellectual aims without imagining social aims as the transitional phase. Yeobright's local peculiarity was that in striving at high thinking he still cleaved to plain living—nay, wild and meagre living in many respects, and brotherliness with clowns. He was a John the Baptist who took ennoblement rather than repentance for his text. Mentally he was in a provincial future, that is, he was in many points abreast with the central town thinkers of his date....
> In consequence of this relatively advanced position, Yeobright might have been called unfortunate. The rural world was not ripe for him. A man should be only partially before his time; to be completely to the vanward in aspirations is fatal to fame....
> A man who advocates aesthetic effort and deprecates social effort is only likely to be understood by a class to which social effort has become a stale matter. To argue upon the possibility of culture

before luxury to the bucolic world may be to argue truly, but it is an attempt to disturb a sequence to which humanity has been long accustomed.

The subtlety and intelligence of this argument from the late 1870s come from a mind accustomed to relative and historical thinking, not merely in the abstract but in the process of observing a personal experience of mobility. This is not country against town, or even in any simple way custom against conscious intelligence. It is the more complicated and more urgent historical process in which education is tied to social advancement within a class society, so that it is difficult, except by a bizarre personal demonstration, to hold both to education and to social solidarity ('he wished to raise the class'). It is the process also in which culture and affluence come to be recognised as alternative aims, at whatever cost to both, and the wry recognition that the latter will always be the first choice, in any real history (as Morris also observed and indeed welcomed).

The relation between the migrant and his former group is then exceptionally complicated. His loyalty drives him to actions which the group can see no sense in, its overt values supporting the association of education with personal advancement which his new group has already made but which for that very reason he cannot accept.

'I am astonished, Clym. How can you want to do better than you've been doing?'

'But I hate that business of mine. . . . I want to do some worthy things before I die.'

'After all the trouble that has been taken to give you a start, and when there is nothing to do but keep straight on towards affluence, you say you . . . it disturbs me, Clym, to find you have come home with such thoughts. . . . I hadn't the least idea you meant to go backward in the world by your own free choice. . . .'

'I cannot help it,' said Clym, in a troubled tone.

'Why can't you do . . . as well as others?'

'I don't know, except that there are many things other people
care for which I don't. . . .'
'And yet you might have been a wealthy man if you had only
persevered. . . . I suppose you will be like your father. Like him,
you are getting weary of doing well.'
'Mother, what is doing well?'

The question is familiar but still after all these years no question
is more relevant or more radical. Within these complex pressures the return of the native has a certain inevitable nullity, and
his only possible overt actions can come to seem merely
perverse. Thus the need for social identification with the
labourers produces Clym's characteristic negative identification
with them; becoming a labourer himself and making his
original enterprise that much more difficult: 'the monotony of
his occupation soothed him, and was in itself a pleasure'.

All this is understood and controlled by Hardy but the
pressure has further and less conscious effects. Levin's choice of
physical labour, in *Anna Karenina*, includes some of the same
motives but in the end is a choosing of people rather than a
choosing of an abstract Nature—a choice of men to work with
rather than a natural force in which to get lost. This crucial
point is obscured by the ordinary discussion of Hardy's attachment to country life, which would run together the 'timeless'
heaths or woods and the men working on them. The original
humanist impulse—'he loved his kind'—can indeed become
anti-human: men can be seen as creatures crawling on this
timeless expanse, as the imagery of the heath and Clym's work
on it so powerfully suggests. It is a very common transition in
the literature of that period but Hardy is never very comfortable with it, and the original impulse, as in *Jude the
Obscure*, keeps coming back and making more precise identi-
fications.

At the same time the separation of the returned native is not only a separation from the standards of the educated and affluent world 'outside'. It is also to some degree inevitably from the people who have not made his journey; or more often a separation which can mask itself as a romantic attachment to a way of life in which the people are merely instrumental: figures in a landscape or when the literary tone fails in a ballad. It is then easy, in an apparently warm-hearted way, to observe for the benefit of others the crudity and limitations but also the picturesqueness, the rough humour, the smocked innocence of 'the bucolic' The complexity of Hardy's fiction shows in nothing more than this: that he runs the whole gamut from an external observation of customs and quaintnesses, modulated by a distinctly patronising affection (as in *Under the Greenwood Tree*), through a very positive identification of intuitions of nature and the values of shared work with human depth and fidelity (as in *The Woodlanders*), to the much more impressive but also much more difficult humane perception of limitations, which cannot be resolved by nostalgia or charm or an approach to mysticism, but which are lived through by all the characters, in the real life to which all belong, the limitations of the educated and the affluent bearing an organic relation to the limitations of the ignorant and the poor (as in parts of *Return of the Native* and in *Tess* and *Jude*). But to make these distinctions and to see the variations of response with the necessary clarity we have to get beyond the stereotypes of the autodidact and the countryman and see Hardy in his real identity: both the educated observer and the passionate participant, in a period of general and radical change.

Hardy's writing, or what in abstraction can be called his style, is obviously affected by the crisis—the return of the native—which I have been describing. We know that he was worried about his prose and was reduced by the ordinary educated assumptions of his period to studying Defoe, Fielding,

Addison, Scott and *The Times*, as if they could have helped him. His complex position as an author, writing about country living to people who almost inevitably saw the country as empty nature or as the working-place of their inferiors, was in any case critical in this matter of language. What have been seen as his strengths—the ballad form of narrative, the prolonged literary imitation of traditional forms of speech—seem to me mainly weaknesses. This sort of thing is what his readers were ready for: a 'tradition' rather than human beings. The devices could not in any case serve his major fiction where it was precisely disturbance rather than continuity which had to be communicated. It would be easy to relate Hardy's problem of style to the two languages of Tess: the consciously educated and the unconsciously customary. But this comparison, though suggestive, is inadequate, for the truth is that to communicate Hardy's experience neither language would serve, since neither in the end was sufficiently articulate: the educated dumb in intensity and limited in humanity; the customary thwarted by ignorance and complacent in habit. The marks of a surrender to each mode are certainly present in Hardy but the main body of his mature writing is a more difficult and complicated experiment. For example:

> The season developed and matured. Another year's instalment of flowers, leaves, nightingales, thrushes, finches, and such ephemeral creatures, took up their positions where only a year ago others had stood in their place when these were nothing more than germs and inorganic particles. Rays from the sunrise drew forth the buds and stretched them into long stalks, lifted up sap in noiseless streams, opened petals, and sucked out scents in invisible jets and breathings.

> Dairyman Crick's household of maids and men lived on comfortably, placidly, even merrily. Their position was perhaps the happiest of all positions in the social scale, being above the line at which neediness ends, and below the line at which the

convenances begin to cramp natural feeling, and the stress of threadbare modishness makes too little of enough.

Thus passed the leafy time when arboresence seems to be the one thing aimed at out of doors. Tess and Clare unconsciously studied each other, ever balanced on the edge of a passion, yet apparently keeping out of it. All the while they were converging, under an irresistible law, as surely as two streams in one vale.

This passage is neither the best nor the worst of Hardy. Rather it shows the many complicated pressures working within what had to seem a single intention. 'The leafy time when arborescence' is an example of mere inflation to an 'educated' style, but the use of *'convenances'*, which might appear merely fashionable, carries a precise feeling. 'Instalment' and 'ephemeral' are also uses of a precise kind, within a sentence which shows mainly the strength of what must be called an educated point of view. The consciousness of the natural process, in 'germs and inorganic particles' (he had of course learned it from Darwin who with Mill was his main intellectual influence) is a necessary accompaniment, for Hardy's purpose, of the more direct and more enjoyed sights and scents of spring. It is loss not gain when Hardy reverts to the simpler and cruder abstraction of 'Dairyman Crick's household of maids and men', which might be superficially supposed to be the countryman speaking but is actually the voice of the detached observer at a low level of interest. The more fully Hardy uses the resources of the whole language, as a precise observer, the more adequate the writing is. There is more strength in 'unconsciously studied each other', which is at once educated and engaged, than in the 'two streams in one vale', which shares with the gesture of 'irresistible law' a synthetic quality, here as of a man playing the countryman novelist.

Hardy's mature style is threatened in one direction by a willed 'Latinism' of diction or construction, of which very many particular instances can be collected (and we have all done it, having taken our education hard), but in the other direction by this much less noticed element of artifice which is too easily accepted, within the patronage we have discussed, as the countryman speaking (sometimes indeed it is literally the countryman speaking, in a contrived picturesqueness which is now the novelist's patronage of his rural characters). The mature style itself is unambiguously an educated style, in which the extension of vocabulary and the complication of construction are necessary to the intensity and precision of the observation which is Hardy's essential position and attribute.

> The gray tones of daybreak are not the gray half-tones of the day's close, though the degree of their shade may be the same. In the twilight of the morning, light seems active, darkness passive; in the twilight of evening, it is the darkness which is active and crescent, and the light which is the drowsy reverse.

This is the educated observer, still deeply involved with the world he is watching, and the local quality of this writing is the decisive tone of the major fiction.

The complication is that this is a very difficult and exposed position for Hardy to maintain. Without the insights of consciously learned history and of the educated understanding of nature and behaviour he cannot really observe at all, at a level of extended human respect. Even the sense of what is now called the 'timeless'—in fact the sense of history, of the barrows, the Roman remains, the rise and fall of families, the tablets and monuments in the churches—is a function of education. That real perception of tradition is available only to the man who has read about it, though what he then sees through it is his native country, to which he is already deeply bound by memory and experience of another kind: a family and a childhood; an intense association of people and places, which has been his own history. To see tradition in both ways is indeed

Hardy's special gift: the native place and experience but also the education, the conscious inquiry. Yet then to see living people, within this complicated sense of past and present, is another problem again. He sees as a participant who is also an observer; this is the source of the strain. For the process which allows him to observe is very clearly in Hardy's time one which includes, in its attachment to class feelings and class separations, a decisive alienation.

> If these two noticed Angel's growing social ineptness, he noticed their growing mental limitations. Felix seemed to him all Church; Cuthbert all College. His Diocesan Synod and Visitations were the mainsprings of the world to the one; Cambridge to the other. Each brother candidly recognized that there were a few unimportant scores of millions of outsiders in civilized society, persons who were neither University men nor Churchmen; but they were to be tolerated rather than reckoned with and respected.

This is what is sometimes called Hardy's bitterness, but in fact it is only sober and just observation. What Hardy sees and feels about the educated world of his day, locked in its deep social prejudices and in its consequent human alienation, is so clearly true that the only surprise is why critics now should still feel sufficiently identified with that world—the world which coarsely and coldly dismissed Jude and millions of other men— to be willing to perform the literary equivalent of that stalest of political tactics: the transfer of bitterness, of a merely class way of thinking, from those who exclude to those who protest. We did not after all have to wait for Lawrence to be shown the human nullity of that apparently articulate world. Hardy shows it convincingly again and again. But the isolation which then follows, while the observer holds to educated procedures but is unable to feel with the existing educated class, is severe. It is not the countryman awkward in his town clothes but the more significant tension—of course with its awkwardness and its spurts of bitterness and nostalgia—of the man caught by his personal history in the general structure and crisis of the relations between education and class, relations which in practice are between intelligence and fellow-feeling. Hardy could not take the James way out, telling his story in a 'spirit of intellectual superiority' to the 'elementary passions'. As he observes again of the Clare brothers:

> Perhaps, as with many men, their opportunities of observation were not so good as their opportunities of expression.

That after all is the nullity, in a time in which education is used to train members of a class and to divide them from other men as surely as from their own passions (for the two processes are deeply connected). And yet there could be no simple going back.

> They had planted together, and together they had felled; together they had, with the run of the years, mentally collected those remoter signs and symbols which seen in few are of runic obscurity, but all together made an alphabet. From the light lashing of the twigs upon their faces when brushing through them in the dark, they could pronounce upon the species of tree whence they stretched; from the quality of the wind's murmur through a bough, they could in like manner name its sort afar off.

This is the language of the immediate apprehension of 'nature', for in that form, always, Hardy could retain a directness of communication. But it is also more specifically the language of shared work, in 'the run of the years', and while it is available as a memory, the world which made it possible is, for Hardy, at a distance which is already enough to detach him: a closeness, paradoxically, that he is still involved with but must also observe and 'pronounce upon'. It is in this sense finally that we must consider Hardy's fundamental attitudes to the country world he was writing about. The tension is not between rural and urban, in the ordinary senses, nor between an abstracted intuition and an abstracted intelligence. The tension, rather, is in his own position, his own lived history, within a general process of change which could come clear and alive in him because it was not only general but in every detail of his feeling observation and writing immediate and particular.

Every attempt has of course been made to reduce the social crisis in which Hardy lived to the more negotiable and detachable forms of the disturbance of a 'timeless order'. But there was nothing timeless about nineteenth-century rural England. It was changing constantly in Hardy's lifetime and before it. It is not only that the next village to Puddletown is Tolpuddle, where you can look from the Martyrs' Tree back to what we know through Hardy as Egdon Heath. It is also that in the 1860s and 1870s, when Hardy was starting to write, it was what he himself described as

> a modern Wessex of railways, the penny post, mowing and reaping machines, union workhouses, lucifer matches, labourers who could read and write, and National school children.

Virtually every feature of this modernity preceded Hardy's own life (the railway came to Dorchester when he was a child of seven). The effects of the changes of course continued. The country was not timeless but it was not static either; indeed, it is because the change was long (and Hardy knew it was long) that the crisis took its particular forms.

We then miss most of what Hardy has to show us if we impose on the actual relationships he describes a pastoral convention of the countryman as an age-old figure, or a vision of a prospering countryside being disintegrated by Corn Law repeal or the railways or agricultural machinery. It is not only that Corn Law repeal and the cheap imports of grain made less difference to Dorset: a county mainly of grazing and mixed farming in which the coming of the railway gave a direct commercial advantage in the supply of milk to London: the economic process described with Hardy's characteristic accuracy in *Tess*:

> They reached the feeble light, which came from the smoky lamp of a little railway station; a poor enough terrestial star, yet in one sense of more importance to Talbothays Dairy and mankind than the celestial ones to which it stood in such humiliating contrast. The cans of new milk were unladen in the rain, Tess getting a little shelter from a neighbouring holly tree. . . .
> . . . 'Londoners will drink it at their breakfasts tomorrow, won't they?', she asked. 'Strange people that we have never seen? . . . who don't know anything of us, and where it comes from, or think how we two drove miles across the moor tonight in the rain that it might reach 'em in time?'

It is also that the social forces within his fiction are deeply based in the rural economy itself: in a system of rent and trade; in the hazards of ownership and tenancy; in the differing conditions of labour on good and bad land and in socially different villages (as in the contrast between Talbothays and Flintcomb Ash); in what happens to people and to families in the interaction between general forces and personal histories—that complex area of ruin or survival, exposure or continuity. This is his actual society, and we cannot suppress it in favour of an external view of a seamless abstracted country 'way of life'.

It is true that there are continuities beyond a dominant social situation in the lives of a particular community (though two or three generations, in a still partly oral culture, can often sustain an illusion of timelessness). It is also obvious that in most rural landscapes there are very old and often unaltered physica features, which sustain a quite different time-scale. Hardy gives great importance to these, and this is not really surprising when we consider his whole structure of feeling. But all these elements are overridden, as for a novelist they must be, by the immediate and actual relationships between people, which occur within existing contemporary pressures and are at most modulated and interpreted by the available continuities.

The pressures to which Hardy's characters are subjected are then pressures from within the system of living, not from outside it. It is not urbanism but the hazard of small-capital farming that changes Gabriel Oak from an independent farmer to a hired labourer and then a bailiff. Henchard is not destroyed by a new and alien kind of dealing but by a development of his own trade which he has himself invited. It is Henchard in Casterbridge who speculates in grain as he had speculated in people; who is in every sense, within an observed way of life, a dealer and a destructive one; his strength compromised by that. Grace Melbury is not a country girl 'lured' by the fashionable world but the daughter of a successful timber merchant whose own social expectations, at this point of his success, include a fashionable education for his daughter. Tess is not a peasant girl seduced by the squire; she is the daughter of a lifeholder and small dealer who is seduced by the son of a retired manufacturer. The latter buys his way into a country house and an old name. Tess's father and, under pressure, Tess herself, are damaged by a similar process, in which an old name and pride are one side of the coin and the exposure of those subject to them the other. That one family fell and one rose is the common and damaging history of what had been happening, for centuries, to ownership and to its consequences in those subject to it. The Lady Day migrations, the hiring fairs, the intellectually arrogant parson, the casual gentleman farmer, the landowner spending her substance elsewhere: all these are as much parts of the country 'way of life' as the dedicated craftsman, the group of labourers and the dances on the green. It is not only that Hardy sees the realities of labouring work, as in Marty South's hands on the spars and Tess in the swede field. It is also that he sees the harshness of economic processes, in inheritance, capital, rent and trade, within the continuity of the natural processes and persistently cutting across them. The social process created in this interaction is one of class and separation, as well as of chronic insecurity, as this capitalist farming and dealing takes its course. The profound disturbances that Hardy records cannot then be seen in the sentimental terms of a pastoral: the contrast between country and town. The exposed and separated individuals, whom Hardy puts at the centre of his fiction, are only the most developed cases of a general exposure and separation. Yet they are never merely illustrations of this change in a way of life. Each has a dominant personal history, which in psychological terms bears a direct relation to the social character of the change.

One of the most immediate effects of mobility, within a structure itself changing, is the difficult nature of the marriage choice. This situation keeps recurring in terms which are at once personal and social: Bathsheba choosing between Bold-wood and Oak; Grace between Giles and Fitzpiers; Jude between Arabella and Sue. The specific class element, and the effects upon this of an insecure economy, are parts of the personal choice which is after all a choice primarily of a way to live, of an identity *in* the identification with this or that other person. And here significantly the false marriage (with which Hardy is so regularly and deeply concerned) can take place either way: to the educated coldness of Fitzpiers or the coarse-ness of Arabella. Here most dramatically the condition of the internal migrant is profoundly known. The social alienation enters the personality and destroys its capacity for any loving fulfilment. The marriage of Oak and Bathsheba is a case of eventual stability, after so much disturbance, but even that has an air of inevitable resignation and lateness. It is true that Hardy sometimes, under pressure, came to generalise and project these very specific failures into a fatalism for which in the decadent thought of his time the phrases were all too ready. In the same way, seeing the closeness of man and the land being broken by the problems of working the land, he sometimes projected his insistence on closeness and continuity into the finally negative images of an empty nature and the tribal past of Stonehenge and the barrows, where the single observer, at least, could feel a direct flow of knowledge. Even these, however, in their deliberate hardness—the uncultivable heath, the bare stone relics—confirm the human negatives, in what looks like a deliberate reversal of pastoral. In them the general alienation has its characteristic monuments, though very distant in time and space from the controlling immediate disturbance.

But the most significant thing about Hardy, in and through these difficulties, is that more than any other major novelist since this difficult mobility began he succeeded, against every pressure, in centring his major novels in the ordinary process of life and work. For all his position as an educated observer, he still took his actions from where the majority of his fellow-countrymen were living. Work enters his novels more decisively than in any English novelist of comparable importance. And it is not merely illustrative; it is seen as it is, as a central kind of learning. Feeling very acutely the long crisis of separation, and in the end coming to more tragically isolated catastrophes than any others within this tradition, he yet created continually the strength and the warmth of people living together: in work and in love; in the physical reality of a place.

To stand working slowly in a field, and feel the creep of rain-water, first in legs and shoulders, then on hips and head, then at back, front, and sides, and yet to work on till the leaden light diminishes and marks that the sun is down, demands a distinct modicum of stoicism, even of valour. Yet they did not feel the wetness so much as might be supposed. They were both young, and they were talking of the time when they lived and loved together at Talbothays Dairy, that happy green tract of land where summer had been liberal in her gifts: in substance to all, emotionally to these.

The general structure of feeling in Hardy would be much less convincing if there were only the alienation, the frustration, the separation and isolation, the final catastrophes. What is defeated but not destroyed at the end of *The Woodlanders* or the end of *Tess* or the end of *Jude* is a warmth, a seriousness, an endurance in love and work that are the necessary definition of what Hardy knows and mourns as loss. Vitally—and it is his difference from Lawrence, as we shall see; a difference of generation and of history but also of character—Hardy does not celebrate isolation and separation. He mourns them, and yet always with the courage to look them steadily in the face. The losses are real and heartbreaking because the desires were real, the shared work was real, the unsatisfied impulses were real. Work and desire are very deeply connected in his whole imagination. That the critical emotional decisions by Tess are taken while she is working—as in the ache and dust of the threshing-machine where she sees Alec again—is no accident of plot; it is how this kind of living connects. The passion of Marty or of Tess or of Jude is a positive force coming out of a working and relating world; seeking in different ways its living fulfilment. That all are frustrated is the essential action: frustrated by very complicated processes of division, separation and rejection. People choose wrongly but under terrible pressures: under the confusions of class, under its misunderstandings, under the calculated rejections of a divided separating world.

It is important enough that Hardy keeps to an ordinary world, as the basis of his major fiction. The pressures to move away from it, to enter a more negotiable because less struggling and less divided life, were of course very strong. And it is even more important, as an act of pure affirmation, that he stays, centrally, with his central figures; indeed moves closer to them in his actual development, so that the affirmation of Tess and of Jude—an affirmation in and through the defeats he traces and mourns—is the strongest in all his work.

Beginning with a work in which he declared his hand—*The Poor Man and the Lady, by the Poor Man*; finding that rejected as mischievous, and getting advice, from Meredith, to retreat into conventional plots; letting the impulse run underground where it was continually disturbing but also always active; gaining a growing certainty which was a strengthening as well as a darkening of vision: Hardy ran his course to an exceptional fidelity.

'Slighted and enduring': not the story of man as he was, distant, limited, picturesque; but slighted in a struggle to grow—to love, to work with meaning, to learn and to teach; enduring in the community of this impulse, which pushes through and beyond particular separations and defeats. It is not only the continuity of a country but of a history that makes me now affirm, with his own certainty and irony: Hardy is our flesh and our grass.

V

A Parting of the Ways

IN 1895 Hardy stopped writing novels. He was to live on and as a major poet until 1928, but there were to be no more novels. *Jude the Obscure* had been hysterically attacked as immoral—

> the experience completely curing me of further interest in novel-writing.

These attacks on *Jude*, as earlier on *Tess*, remind us of something we now easily forget: that of all nineteenth-century novelists Hardy was the most bitterly received, in his important work, by the English establishment. He is in this sense a true predecessor—though it is a lineage none of them wanted—of Joyce and Lawrence.

Hardy's stopping novel-writing was, of course, more complicated than that. But the date, 1895, can serve to indicate as well as single dates ever can a new situation in the English novel. I don't mean only that it feels like the end of that great nineteenth-century realist tradition. In a way we must not cut that off: the continuity from Hardy to Lawrence is central. But between *Jude the Obscure* and *Sons and Lovers* there is in effect a generation: a missing generation. Yet what happened between the 1890s and 1914 is of great critical importance for the novel. It is a period of crisis and of a parting of the ways. The different roads then taken and the disputes that accompanied each creative choice connect in important ways to our own world. Some of the problems then raised we still haven't resolved. Indeed the central problem—the relation between what separated out as 'individual' or 'psychological' fiction on the one hand and 'social' or 'sociological' fiction on the other—is still, though perhaps in new ways, at the heart of our creative difficulties and concerns.

At the same time, as a lesser matter than that creative difficulty but of course affecting it (as a critical context, a critical vocabulary, inevitably does) we have to face the fact that academically, professionally the choice of roads has been overridden by a marked and settled preference. The fiction that emerged from one of these roads, from the 1890s to the 1920s, is still, oddly—it is even odder when Lawrence has somehow to be reconciled with it—recommended as 'modern'. It tells us a lot about contemporary Britain that 'modern' is that period of our grandfathers and great-grandfathers. But the record got stuck just there and it's been very difficult, for reasons we may see, to jerk it going again. That critical celebration of the 'modern' is, as you know, self-perpetuating and thriving.

Of course when I said there was a gap between Hardy and Lawrence you must have immediately been filling it in. The names are all there: James and Conrad; the early novels of Forster, indeed all but *A Passage to India*; and then of course that composite figure H. G. A. J. Wells-Bennett-Galsworthy, Esquire. It's all these I want to discuss (though I shall concentrate more specifically on Conrad later). Not because in taking them together I can hope to say enough that is specific and relevant to each particular writer; but because it is even more important, I think—important as a way of taking some decisive bearings—to see what the choices were, what the effects and consequences were; and to make this examination active, not just as so often a critical play-off of one group over another. The point of my argument, I can say now, is that the division of roads, the choices and the effects of the choices, are much too serious and complicated for that familiar demonstration and putting down. Virginia Woolf's essay *Mr Bennett and Mrs*

Brown can be printed on vellum and given away as a presentation copy to anybody whose mind is already made up about those fateful issues (though perhaps not, it would cost a fortune given ordinary critical inertia). In any case I want to try to show that the issues are still very active and undecided; the issues I mean as they connect to our own active world.

1895. I've argued before that in the late 1870s, the early 1880s, the Victorian period ended. Of course the Queen lived on and it's not her fault but ours, our particular muddle, if we choose to describe our history by these single anointed lives. Socially, culturally, economically, politically, a new phase of our history began. It is quite identifiable, from the late 1870s to the war in 1914. And what is there as scattered accumulating evidence, over two decades, reaches a critical point in the 1890s. The last year of Hardy, the year of *Jude the Obscure*, is also the first year of Wells, the year of *The Time Machine*. Henry James covers the whole period of this visibly altering world. The important and characteristic critical quarrel between them, between Wells and James, reached its decisive point at the very end of the period, between 1911 and 1914. It is that world, that emerging deciding dividing world, that I want first to stress.

And here it is necessary to argue that in many other ways—other ways than in fiction—something important and decisive was happening in that period to what can be called the English tradition. Coming myself from a border area I'm always uneasy about these national names. I have to look both ways, over both shoulders at once. English literature; the English novel: these are literature, novels, in English; and there is already before this period, and increasingly important after it, the significant and creative work of American writers in English to be added but as a tradition—a vital tradition—in itself. All through the literature, men from other parts of the culture than the specifically English have contributed: Scots, Irish, Welsh. But on the whole, in the nineteenth-century novel, there is a very specific Englishness. Marian Evans had border connections, but her county is Warwickshire. The Brontës were Bruntys in County Down only a generation before the novelists, but the generation is all that now matters. Disraeli, yes; that's a case on its own but I'd settle for Beaconsfield, as he did; that's how the consciousness went. Meredith—I have to pronounce him in that English way because for him that is how it was, though in Wales the sound is quite different; Meredith the Englishman. And Dickens, Thackeray, Trollope, Elizabeth Gaskell, Thomas Hardy: English, English specifically. It isn't the origins that matter. It's the common consciousness, the common culture; a very specific set of common concerns, common preoccupations. Disturbed certainly; profoundly disturbed; that's what I've mainly been arguing. But with a creative confidence, a creative centre, that is there and impressive, continuously impressive: the English, specifically English, novel.

It's not been like that since and of course there are many reasons. Out of the profound disturbance from the 1830s to the 1870s something new was fashioned; something more openly confident, more settled, less rough at the edges; something English in a new sense, where many of the real difficulties begin. It appears in many ways but I'd settle for saying the formed self-confident insulated middle class. That class you could see coming, hear coming, all the way through the century, but now arrived and housed, settled in. The *English* middle class, English in a new sense—insulated and strong in their insulation just because, perhaps, that island within an island ruled an Empire, ruled half a world.

It's the point, as it happens, where English for me becomes problematic. I don't belong, don't wish to belong, to what English then means. But of course I respect it, I've had to, for some of the real things it is. In science particularly it is a superb culture; and in the technical and learned and administrative professions if not superb at least strong. But its weakness, its very deep weakness, is in ideas and imagination: not from some national quality, disquality—I don't accept that for a moment; it's untrue and unreal. It was in imagination and ideas, from Blake to Hardy and from Coleridge to Morris, that the specific greatness of something identifiably English—and English of the period after the Industrial Revolution, carrying on what was already a major imaginative and intellectual culture—was founded. But weak, problematic, at that particular time and in that particular place: the last decades of the nineteenth century, the first decade of our own.

It was, we must remember, a dominant culture, meant to be dominant, filtering other cultures, other classes, through its own curious mesh, and there again, clogging the mesh a bit, a new self-conscious experimental minority; getting out of line, speaking out of turn, bohemians and artists. Before that settlement, with all its supporting and interlocking and modernised institutions, much of the really creative work had come from other groups: from women, who had been very specifically excluded from the forming masculine world (the importance of women novelists in the nineteenth century is well known and remarkable); from mobile individuals, with what were called lower or lower-middle class associations—Carlyle, Dickens, Hardy. But in the new period this is much more marked; is indeed almost exclusive. And a new element enters that through the twentieth century—at least till the second war—stood out quite remarkably. Yeats, Shaw, Joyce, Synge, O'Casey; Henry James, T. S. Eliot, Pound; Conrad. Other nationalities, other conscious nationalities, and from these immigrants, these outsiders, the major imaginative work. Of course this is in part a response to Empire, just as the figures for genius in fifth-century Athens have to be qualified by where those figures came from to that decisive centre. But it's more than that. It's the cultural question that from this time on gets more and more asked: where, by the way, are the English? Well, Lawrence was to come, as Carlyle and Dickens and Hardy had come. But in this settling period, apart from Mr Forster, there is only that enigmatic figure Wells-Bennett-Galsworthy. And it's worth reflecting—indeed it's necessary to reflect— how much of the reaction against him, against them, has to do with a version, a subsequent version, of how narrow how un- imaginative how upholstered and materialist the English—the English!—had become.

This fact of mobility and of alternative viewpoints comes profoundly, in this period, to affect the novel. There's a crisis I've been tracing through all the novelists so far, in their different ways: a crisis of language and form, a tension within language and form, which now comes to a new phase. In effect, I'd say, what had been a tension became now a split. Internal disturbances of the sort we saw in George Eliot and in Hardy became too strong, too restless, to be contained any longer within any single writer (though Lawrence tried, and we shall see what a struggle it was, what in the end it cost him).

Internal disturbances of language and form. But these, I've been saying all along, are problems of relationship, of essential relationship: to and with other people, other groups, other classes; but as these work through in any real experience dis- turbances of consciousness, the consciousness of the writer. Educated and customary, public and private—these are settling terms, quietening terms, for what were really, in all the most interesting, the most exposed minds, not definitions or cate- gories but moving continuous and unconscious histories. And it wasn't that the new minds were any less serious. What they had to hold to, had to try to see whole, was in itself more com- plicated, more deeply dividing and disturbing.

It was not, for example, a less divided society in the 1890s than in the Two Nations of the 1840s. It was more advanced and more prosperous but it was also more rationally, more objectively and consciously and functionally divided.

> The great house, the church, the village, and the labourers and the servants in their stations and degrees, seemed to me, I say, to be a closed and complete social system. About us were other villages and great estates, and from house to house, interlacing, correlated, the Gentry, the fine Olympians, came and went.... I thought this was the order of the whole world. . . . It seemed to be in the divine order.

That's Wells, in *Tono Bungay*, on that Bladesover world in which his mother was a servant. Of course, if it were only that, it would be nothing new. It's the world Jane Austen described, the world George Eliot extended and then under pressure went back to for the ideas, for the talk. But Wells goes on:

> That all this fine appearance was already sapped, that there were forces at work that might presently carry all this elaborate social system in which my mother instructed me so carefully that I might understand my place, to Limbo, had scarcely dawned upon me. . . .

And that's the real point: the consciousness, the gathering consciousness of the end of a period; but of an end within something 'closed and complete', something externally solid and absolute.

> It is like an early day in a fine October. The hand of change rests on it all, unfelt, unseen; resting for awhile, as it were half reluctantly, before it grips and ends the thing for ever. One frost and the whole face of things will be bare. . . .

Or again, to explain and define, a new note: a new consciousness, self-consciousness of the 'modern':

> England was all Bladesover two hundred years ago; . . . it has had reform Acts indeed, and such-like changes of formula, but no essential revolution since then; . . . all that is modern and

different has come in as a thing intruded or as a gloss upon this predominant formula, either impertinently or apologetically.

It is the important Wells tone: something now easily, too easily dismissed; overt and challenging, set up like a milepost along a brand new road that hasn't yet been built. Yet what he says is obviously true, even of his own way of saying it:

all that is modern and different has come in as a thing intruded or as a gloss. . . .

For the predominant formula at the time he was writing was not only a traditional community—the country-house world of Bladesover. It was also the inherited, the shaping form of the novel.

Now it is here, really, that the split takes place. To accept that world, that form, was in a very deep way to accept its consciousness. Of course with every kind of qualification and refinement; an intense pressure, a self-conscious and intricate pressure within that imaginary, imaginative circle. To question the circle itself, to examine the relations which composed it—profound relations of property, income, work, education—was not only radical in overt ways—asking radical questions, giving radical opinions. It was a break in texture where consciousness itself was determined; an assault, or so it seemed, not only on the form of the novel but on an idea, *the* idea, of literature itself.

And this is Wells's importance, and the real significance of his quarrel with James. You've only to read the introduction to their exchanges—a modern introduction, by critical minds set firmly on one side of this argument, a set that goes almost too deep to be noticed—you've only to notice the tones, the terms, their familiarity in contemporary discussion, to see how central this difference is. To break out from Bladesover once you were really aware of it was to break every convention at once. It had been different for Hardy, away from that Home Counties, that determining world. Hardy lived still where England was active in all its main senses: a working relating society. That's why of course, very quickly, he was called—'placed' as—a regional novelist; or to take the word that was really to turn the trick, provincial. All that was not Home Counties—meaning that social formation that stretched from St James's to places like Bladesover but also to Calcutta and Boston—all the places and feelings of another England were provincial; let it have, in a folk way, its regional, its provincial works. But where consciousness was formed—in the schools, the colleges, the clubs, the country-houses—nobody supposed himself in the presence of a sector, a sect; he was now at the centre, the centre of the world; and a centre that could take over with its trained confidence all that England had been, all that literature had been.

Of course, at very different levels: all the way from *The Spoils of Poynton* to Galsworthy's *The Country House*. That's what's wrong, by the way, about that composite figure Wells-Bennett-Galsworthy. Bennett in all the work that matters, the very fine early work, is a located, that is to say an English novelist. The link, it might have been, from George Eliot and Hardy to Lawrence, who was very aware of him. But in this new phase, and of course in himself, without the staying-power, without the persistent creative autonomy: drawn in, sucked in, pushing in to that consuming reconciling centre. And Galsworthy was inside it from the beginning. Galsworthy writing that intensive internal study formally after Turgeniev, but Turgeniev was an exile, a real exile, and that made all the difference. Galsworthy, certainly, is self-critical, what is called satirical, but within limits of course: within that centre's limits. The farthest he really gets is the division, the superficial division, that was possible inside it: between business people and artistic people; conventional people and promiscuous people; sheep and black sheep. It's the same kind of novel only the tensions are all on the surface; not working, not disturbing but set—often effectively and memorably—in prepared situations, contrasting characters. And past these arranged confrontations, with their steady implication of change and reform, is a deciding continuity: a sense that this and only this is the human scale.

And then Wells is very different. He failed in the end; he emigrated to World Government as clearly as Lawrence to Mexico. But until 1914, until that real break that went beyond him, not only a restless energy—fashion is prepared to concede that to outsiders—but a creative energy, and a creative energy in fiction. His simplest successes are of course what are called the romances (that's placing again, very like 'provincial'). He avoids tearing that seamless cloth, that traditional texture of the novel, by taking his consciousness of change—his sense of history and of the urgency of transformation—outside that social fiction, that intensive realism, where in existing circumstances such questions could never be put; or rather, could be put as questions but could never become actions. The Morlocks and the Eloi at the end of the Time Machine; the alteration of consciousness in the passing of the Comet; the disturbance of conventions by the invisible man: these were real ways through, in an otherwise reconciling world. Kipps and Mr Polly, men on the run from the system: there we see the alternative: an irrepressible humour and energy, but not the humour and energy of Dickens, transforming a world; only the endlessly self-conscious, self-consciously perky, the almost apologetic assertion—over the shoulder, behind the hand—of a right to live.

I can feel with this strongly, as I felt strongly with Lewisham many years ago making schedules for exams: the first character in fiction I ever clearly identified with. But it's a game, you know (to revert to the idiom): only a game, old man. Like

Orwell's Mr Bowling thirty years later in *Coming Up for Air*,
it's a dog off leash; a gay dog, a sad dog. More like us, much
more like us, that any Forsyte or Warburton, but still only in
odd corners or doing a public act—a public act among friends.
And nostalgic always, cosily nostalgic: an adolescent nostalgia,
a whole world away from the bitter and tearing—yet then
profoundly connecting—adult memories of George Eliot or
Hardy or Lawrence. Of course we all wish there were a little
pub by the river, where we could live and let live. We wish it
when we're tired, or when general change is too hard or too
disturbing. It's the appealing side, the nice side, of the petit
bourgeois; with the emphasis on the small man, the little
human peninsula, trying to forget what the high bourgeois
mainland is like (and in that turning away there's some genuine
warmth).

What it grows up into, unfortunately, is that consciousness
Wells really does share with Bennett, and that's been very
pervasive: a bouncing cheeky finally rampant commercialism:
not Mr Polly but Northcliffe, and beyond him the *Daily
Mirror* and ITV; the break-out—what's called a break-out—
from Bladesover to Tono Bungay. It's because of this, I suppose,
that the ghosts of Henry James and of Matthew Arnold are still
so regularly summoned: an enclosed and intricate lamplit
seriousness against all that cheerful bounce that so quickly
becomes a mechanical thump, practically breaking your
shoulder. It's a measure of our difficulty that we think it's
there—only there—we've got to choose.

Yet what an odd thing it is that we have to say this about
Wells, who could see worlds transformed, entire systems
changed, a modern Utopia. That's the key of course: that last
word, Utopia. Wells is unique in his time because he saw very
clearly the scale of the change that was coming, the change that
had to be fought for. He couldn't bring it together in any single

form: the world as it is and the scale of the change. But he exploits the distance, the imaginative distance, with a skill that's the basis of both his comedy and his prophetics. It's a now familiar experience: the difference between the pace of history and the pace of a life: the difference, I mean, in deeply established, deeply customary and yet resourceful societies. We oughtn't to take too seriously his final abandonment of literature—I mean when he says he doesn't want it, can't use it, would rather write something else. We oughtn't to take this too seriously as a way of dismissing him, as a way of dismissing his problem, as it's possible to do if you think in conventional ways that you know what literature is, what that seamless texture is, what that circle—that conventional circle—encloses. Ever since Wells and still with real difficulty and urgency we have seen a confusion of forms, an overlapping of interests, a formal separation of imagination, social criticism and documentary which in practice keeps breaking down as the real interests rejoin. And the interaction of the interests (the older name of course is just general human experience) is where literature, inevitably, is.

What we have then to try to say, as precisely and as justly as we can, is what happened to literature, to that seamless literature, through all this disturbance. And we can only do this seriously if we acknowledge the disturbance; acknowledge, I mean, its necessity, its reality. If we say the disturbance is some system, call it sociology or materialism or technologico-Benthamism, we gain some rhetorical victories but at a terrible cost; at the expense, really, of any continuing literature, though with a residual emphasis—a very pure emphasis—on the achieved literature, the decided literature of the past. For the questions that fired Wells—very similar questions, for all the difference of tone, to the questions that fired Lawrence, and that are still very close to us—were necessary questions, running back to the disturbances of Dickens and George Eliot and Hardy.

What a stable society, a known civilisation, most evidently offers is a human emphasis, a place for human emphasis. Given that stability we can look long and deep; look at human possibility, at individual strengths and weaknesses, always intricately meshed with each other; look, examine, with a seriousness that depends, really, on certain other possibilities having been ruled out: say war, poverty, revolutionary conflict. The change of the novel in the mid-nineteenth century had been a change made necessary by just these disturbances: a sudden and desperate realisation of what was really at stake in all our active relationships.

This realisation came again at the turn of the century: as urgently, as unavoidably as in that generation of the 1840s, but now, we must see, with very different results. The new social and historical consciousness was more general, necessarily general, because the scale had widened. It wasn't only a crisis within a single society, a nation: that specific Englishness which was a strength, a focus, in the generation from Dickens to Hardy. Much wider issues, implicit before, now became explicit: war and imperialism, which then had been distant or marginal; poverty and revolution, which had new international bearings. It was a very much longer way—impossibly longer it seemed and can still seem—from those human crises, crises that do decide life, to what can be known directly and particularly as human crisis: that experience, that relationship—visible, tangible experience and relationship; the texture of what James so rightly called, emphasised as 'felt life'.

Not that war, imperialism, poverty, revolution were other than life; were simply abstractions called politics. 'Something other than human life': that phrase of Blake's is not to be transplanted, not when we really think of Blake, to processes which in the generations now living were to make their way into every experience and every relationship directly and indirectly, as George Eliot had foreseen. What I call the split, between the 1890s and the first war, was in a way inevitable; only a far-reaching change could have prevented it. But it is from that time on and especially in the novel that people tried to talk of 'social' and 'personal' as separable processes, separate realms. 'Social'—we've all seen it—became the pejorative 'sociological', and a 'sociological' interest was in 'something other than human life', in classes, statistics, abstract ideas, systems. 'Personal'—we may have noticed this less—became the whole of 'human'; the recommending, ratifying 'human'— love, friendship, marriage, death. And you can now very quickly start a fight anywhere between the claims of the definitions: which of the two is really substantial, decisive, important, significant. Schools clash or more often ignore and despise each other. 'Sociological' is a sneer you may think the last word until you hear 'literary' from the other side of the fence. Systems of all kinds (and this is really odd) rise to support each principality. The deciding reality is here, or here. False consciousness and superstructure, rationalisation and projection are the names for what the others are doing, for all they are doing. And at this new frontier, the writer can seem to be required to present himself with a clear identity paper: is he poet or sociologist? interested in literature or in politics? committed to reality or to the merely incidental and personal? What had been always precariously a republic of letters became this series of jealous and squabbling states and areas; in the end down to fields. And in the process, unnoticed, the seamless cloth of literature had been simply, impudently carried off.

I don't mean carried off by James: not in his work anyway, though the critical prefaces are different. It's very easy to raise, even to feel a prejudice against James: as Wells let it out in *Boon*—

> every light and line focused on the high altar. And on the altar, very reverently placed, intensely there, is a dead kitten, an eggshell, a piece of string.

That won't do at all, won't survive a few minutes' re-reading of James himself. Very serious human actions are at the centre of all his best work, and this means most of it. Very serious and material actions, as it happens. It is a much more materialist fiction than Wells, who is idealist, fantasist, to the core. James tells us how he would rewrite in his mind almost everybody he read; he even did this—it's a thought—to Wells' *First Men in the Moon*. But what he could really rewrite, what belongs in his dimension and would be much improved by it, is Galsworthy: that's where the conventional groupings really break down. He hasn't Galsworthy's interest in remedy, that is to say in change. He has excluded from the novel as any major element not morality, moralising (though people praise that exclusion, are glad to be free of didacticism, welcome the wrought work of life—art—that is there and wholly known). Any knowing, any showing, any *presentation*—to take the exact word for James—is moral inevitably. The selection and the placing are the judgments, of a sort that could be made especially by someone in his position; someone not in ordinary ways himself at stake and involved. But what he has really excluded is history: that other dimension of value which from Scott through Dickens and George Eliot and Hardy to Lawrence (but not to Joyce) has transformed prose fiction.

Some of the deepest and also some of the coarsest human problems are at the centre of James's work: people using each other, betraying, failing, destroying: not a small world in that sense, and certainly not relics or eggshells. Since an image has been offered I will suggest my own. Not an altar, there's nothing reverent. Past the qualifying assuaging oblique tone it's the reverse of reverent; even cruel when you get to the heart. But I remember that first scene in George Eliot's *Daniel Deronda*— that novel which in one of its parts has been rightly seen as a lead to James: that scene in

> one of those splendid resorts which the enlightenment of ages has prepared . . . a suitable condenser for human breath belonging, in great part, to the highest fashion . . . the atmosphere . . . well-brewed to a visible haze.

What is happening is gambling, 'dull gas-poisoned absorption', though there is a detached observer and a little boy looking away towards the door. But that image of a table at which people come to play, making moves of the utmost seriousness and intricacy in which their lives are staked though the tone is still of a diversion, and with an imaginary circle cutting them off, really cutting them off, not only from where the money is made but from where the lives are made in direct relationship, in creation, in the real and connected care of life: that table, full of absorbed players speaking a language of their own, and the clear-eyed observer, seeing the game, the haze, so exactly, and the boy looking away to the door: that for me— I mean as an image—is the actual James world.

And this is why, I think, his art is so fine of its kind. The concentration, the working, are very remarkable. I have often thought reading James—*The Portrait of a Lady* is still the best example—that human speech in its intricacy, its particularity, its quality as a sequence, has never been better rendered. That it is the speech of a class makes, at first, little difference; all languages are in some sense particular. But then what also strikes me is that it is just this working, this rendering, that is the defining centre. I don't mean the defining of others, I mean the rendering, the preoccupied rendering, of a single reality 'well-brewed to a visible haze'. In James, that is to say, and the effect of this is very important, the emphasis has so shifted within an apparently continuous form—it is an emphasis that began to change, as I've argued, in George Eliot—that we call two kinds of fiction, two kinds of novel, by the same generic name—'psychological realism', when what has really happened is a transfer of process from the signified to the signifier; from the material to the work on material; from the life to the art.

The art, let's say quickly, is also life—that distinction won't ever really do except as a first approximation. The act of seeing, the act of making, the act of rendering and presenting is life itself of an intense kind. But of a kind, undoubtedly; a kind 'psychological realism' doesn't describe, define closely enough or perhaps define at all. What really matters in James is that act of signifying in which the novel becomes its own subject, as opposed to late Wells, in which the subject, the isolated subject, becomes the novel. Consciousness in James, to put it another way, is the almost exclusive object and subject of consciousness. This is the source of the perceptive brilliance and the ease of James's stories about writing and writers: *The Lesson of the Master*, *The Figure in the Carpet* or the relaxed connecting *Death of a Lion* or *The Next Time*. But in the larger works it's a thing in itself, and of course it reveals a great deal. Not a solipsist fiction. On the contrary. That's where the separation, the wrenching-apart of 'individual' and 'society' comes in to confuse us. Since consciousness is social its exploration, its rendering as a process, is connecting, inevitably. The figures that form there, figures of consciousness—of this or that done or said— are as moving, as connecting, as recognised as any figures in the world. More recognised we might even say; more tangible, tactile, by a curious paradox: more undeniably *there*—to come back to that word—than the figures less brewed in that visible haze; figures—but then not figures, men and women—who might get up and walk away, who are not accessible, not accessible and workable in that way, to the ever-conscious, not involved but absorbed novelist.

It's this, in the end, I mean by the split. Not just 'social' realism or 'psychological' realism, though that's a way of putting it: a pulling of life, in the scale and complexity of any now known community, one way or the other—their overt common acts in their social identities; or their unexpressed desires, attachments, movements in their personal identities. In the next generation it settled down like that: one kind of reality or the other seemed to have to be chosen. But in this decisive period it is still a problem of relationship, of the writer's relationship: what Wells hits (among many misses) when he says James relates before everything to 'The Novel'.

It comes out in another way as we see James's critical preferences, James's selection and rejection of ancestors: the tradition he tried to establish, though it sometimes embarrasses its subsequent propagandists. Flaubert: 'for many of our tribe at large *the* novelist' (and notice 'tribe'; the writing community is now the most known, the most knowable; that is the radical change). Flaubert's complications

> were of the spirit, of the literary vision, and though he was thoroughly profane he was yet essentially anchoretic.

That has a characteristic (if comically edged) brilliance; it is very exactly, very referentially said. 'The spirit . . . the literary vision.' But Dickens: *Bleak House, Little Dorrit, Our Mutual Friend*—'forced . . . laboured . . . dug out as with a spade and pickaxe' (the metaphors of work, in that tone, are precisely revealing). Or again:

> A story based upon those elementary passions in which alone we seek the true and final manifestation of character must be told in a spirit of intellectual superiority to those passions.

'Intellect' and 'passions': that's one way of putting it, and the point about the 'spirit of intellectual superiority' is certainly relevant. We've been haunted by that spirit, often in obviously borrowed or ill-fitting clothes, through so many of the corridors of literary education.

But it's not really a matter of faculties of the mind; it's a relationship, 'intellect' and 'passions', between a novelist and 'his' characters; the relationship I was defining in George Eliot and Hardy; between the novelist and other people, at that depth where a society—a knowable society—is at issue and is decided.

The most critical reference is to Tolstoy:

the great illustrative master-hand on all this ground of disconnection of method from matter.

And Wells and Bennett are seen as Tolstoy's 'diluted' successors. It sounds like a critical point; what is now usually taken as a critical point, something about 'method' and 'matter'. But it is the terms that are revealing, since the relationship James senses in Tolstoy—the relationship that disturbs and indeed ought to disturb him—is not a matter of 'art' in his sense at all. It is a matter of relationship between the writer and other men (and so between the writer and his work, himself). There's a subsidiary answer, if you feel you have to find one. Tolstoy works, creates, puts an intense life there, with a range and a power of sustained attention against which James, obviously, is minor. But that's not the main point. Tolstoy couldn't accept that version of consciousness, of relationship, which was becoming—exclusively, even arrogantly—'literature': that working, working over, working through, by the last of the great men, the last hero, the novelist, the signifier. For always beyond that lighted circle, that imaginative circle, was a stubborn active connecting life: not 'matter' at all, and always challenging the preoccupation—the *preoccupation*—with 'method'. So that 'social' and 'personal', 'public' and 'private', 'historical' and 'psychological' make no sense in Tolstoy: make no sense of him in his sustained, his truly preoccupying and connecting life and art. The continuum of experience: that's one way of putting it. But it's never passive, never given. It's an active relationship, an exploration into consciousness which at its most intricate and intimate is a consciousness of others, and of others with us in history, in production, in the care and maintenance of life. Not matter then to be absorbed by a method; but an experience almost breaking, needing to break, any available signifying form; and yet in and through itself, in the pressure and structure of active experience, creating forms, creating life: *the* novelist, in and outside the tribe.

And when that pressure and struggle became too intense— too intense, I mean, in a society suspended, temporarily dominant, unable to change—there was a falling away into alternative concerns. Or concerns seen as alternative: the issues of history and society—what Wells went on to write about, to set up as props in his novels; or the close issues of personal life— what a late bourgeois literature, though not yet in full flight, selected, deliberately selected, as the only knowable reality, the only known and yet inevitably excluding community. There's no choice in the end between those two roads; no separable merit—I mean merit in emphasis—in either. It's like the choice, the related choice—the same choice in other terms—between art as a vehicle, the position Wells came to argue, and art as autonomous in its own clear circle, the position of James. That, it seems to me, is no choice at all: the terms, the questions, are just records of a failure. But as we put it that way, let's take care, respecting care, to emphasise the seriousness, the effort, the important and lasting energy of the attempt to keep hold, to keep going. In Forster, for example, we can see these radical impulses straining almost dislocating his early novels; the sense of strain, of inevitable but reluctant divergence as late as *A Passage to India*, and then the significant silence in this most honest, most self-appraising of our living writers. But the larger energies of Wells and of James—those figures who force us, forced each other, to an eventual contrast—these energies remind us of how much was at stake; of what a crisis it was, in that time, that period, that now wrongly seems static.

It is history now. The choices don't come in that open way again and what succeeds the division, the parting of the ways, is a renewal of energy, a renewal of the novel, as important as anything that preceded it. It's just that criticism, literary history hasn't really caught up; has taken the terms of that split and continued to apply them as a sort of prescription—actually a biased prescription, a symptom—when the real sickness is the separation into classes, into categories, into mutually hostile preoccupations and methods: the individual *or* society; public *or* private; social *or* literary studies.

What matters to us is the crisis itself: where what was and is most creative in the novel—the open response to an extending and active society, the similarly open response to intense and unique and connecting feeling—encountered major difficulties: difficulties of relationship and so difficulties of form: difficulties that connect and disturb through all the rest of our century.

VI

Joseph Conrad

ISOLATION and struggle. Man against Fate. These have been the common terms of descriptions of Conrad. And of course they are relevant. The novels raise those issues. But I want to look at the phrases and at the ideas behind them—turn them round and look at them—because I am far from sure that in the end with Conrad they help; at least in their simple rhetorical forms. There is isolation in Conrad of course. There is Man and there is Fate: the abstractions and others like them are a critical part of his style. And of course there is struggle of an intense kind: more intense, more practical, for many reasons, then in most other novelists in the language. But when we put the terms together, as in the ordinary account, are we still with Conrad in any central way? Is it quite that world, that metaphysical world, that his novels compose?

We have to make discriminations between and within his work, if we are to answer that question. Take first, as he did, the stories of the sea and of ships. There if anywhere, we might say, are the physical instances of the metaphysical situation. There very clearly men can find themselves alone against overwhelming forces, natural forces. The sea can feel like an enemy: incomprehensible, implacable.

> The ship trembled from trucks to keel; the sails kept on rattling like a discharge of musketry; the chain sheets and loose shackles jingled aloft in a thin peal; the gin blocks groaned. It was as if an invisible hand had given the ship an angry shake to recall the men that peopled her decks to the sense of reality, vigilance and duty.

140

'As if an invisible hand'. It is a way Conrad often writes.

> The ship knew, and sometimes would correct the presumptuous human ignorance by the wholesome discipline of fear.

Yet this is never the only emphasis.

> Singleton didn't stir. A long while after he said, with unmoved face:—'Ship! . . . Ships are all right. It is the men in them.'

And the angry shake of the invisible hand, we remember, was to recall the men to a sense of 'reality, vigilance and duty'. To recall men, that is to say, to the fact of their existence as a ship's company, a working community.

Or take that famous case of isolation: the isolation of Lord Jim. What actually isolates him? What is he really struggling against? There is certainly the storm that threatens the *Patna*. But the central crisis is very human and social. Jim has been taught a code, a set of laws about sailing, and these are not only technical but in their essence moral—definitions of responsibility and of duty which are at once specific practical rules and general social laws. He is a part of a hierarchy—the officers of the ship—in which those laws are manifest or are supposed to be manifest. His moral conflict is not the product of isolation, of the lack of a society and of shared beliefs. It is that earlier kind of conflict, historically earlier, in which a man's strength is tested under pressure; in which others break the agreed rules and he goes along with this to his subsequent shame; in which, that is to say, what is really being looked at is *conduct*, within an agreed scheme of values.

The ship in Conrad has this special quality, which was no longer ordinarily available to most novelists. It is a knowable community of a transparent kind. The ship has in the main a clear and shared social purpose and an essentially unquestioned customary morality, expressed in fellow-feeling and in law. Within these terms Conrad can write with a simplicity and clarity of moral emphasis that may appear when taken outside this very specific community merely abstract or verbal.

No community of this kind is in fact without conflict. *The Nigger of the 'Narcissus'* is a struggling community in so many ways: the crew struggling against the sea, struggling with each other, and within all their active relationships failing to recognise the truth about the Nigger, which their roughness hides. Nevertheless:

> Haven't we, together and upon the immortal sea, wrung out a meaning from our sinful lives? Goodbye, brothers!

Like any active community the ship's company learns from experience and consequence. Even its heroes, like Captain MacWhirr in *Typhoon*, are a kind of consummation of this shared strength. The isolated man taking his ship through the typhoon is an instance, an heroic instance, of essentially shared values:

> Facing it—always facing it—that's the way to get through. You are a young sailor. Face it. That's enough for any man. Keep a cool head.

It is this that men have learned, face to face with natural forces:

> The hurricane, with its power to madden the seas, to sink ships, to uproot trees, to overturn strong walls and dash the very birds of the air to the ground, had found this taciturn man in its path, and, doing its utmost, had managed to wring out a few words.

The individual heroism is a clear social value, a way of living and sailing.

But of course even the close community of the ship is not really isolated. The strength and skill of seamanship, of the ship's company, are always necessary, but the purpose of the voyage, the seaworthiness of the vessel, responsibilities to families or to owners, begin and end on land, in a more complicated society. The conflicts of value which then inevitably

occur involve different viewpoints and a different consciousness.

> He had attended faithfully, as by law a shipmaster is expected to
> do, to the conflicting interests of owners, charterers and under-
> writers. He had never lost a ship or consented to a shady trans-
> action; and he had lasted well, outlasting in the end the conditions
> that had gone to the making of his name.

That is Captain Whalley in *The End of the Tether*. But it is not
these known conflicts that wreck him. In his own capacity he
has steered his life straight during fifty years at sea. But

> he had buried his wife (in the Gulf of Petchili), had married off
> his daughter to the man of her unlucky choice, and had lost more
> than an ample competence in the crash of the notorious Travan-
> core and Deccan Banking Corporation, whose downfall had
> shaken the East like an earthquake. And he was sixty-seven years
> old.

Whalley is going blind, but under pressure to send money to
his daughter he tries to use his experience to continue in
command. The ambitious, 'instinctively disloyal' Sterne dis-
covers his secret and deliberately wrecks him. But he couldn't
have done this if Whalley had not already broken the only law
he has lived by: that responsibility which now another responsibility contradicts.

> This necessity opened his eyes to the fundamental changes of the
> world.

Or again Lord Jim, after the crisis of the *Patna* where what is
abandoned is not only a ship but the eight hundred 'unconscious pilgrims of an exacting belief', has to relive his choice of
duty at the edge of the colonial world, in the complicated and
peripheral society of merchants, brigands, native rulers, the
interaction of economies and of cultures. Without leaving the
world of the ship, but simply following its natural extensions
in trade and its consequences, Conrad pushes towards what is in

the end the heart of darkness. There is an immense regret, and an altered tone, as 'lawful trade'—the simple social definition to which the laws of seamanship could directly relate—is seen in its real complications. Over much of this seeing the simpler values still preside. A man who has known the crew of the '*Narcissus*' is not going to be surprised by the people around Patusan, and in the first instance he will know exactly how to describe them. But in *The Heart of Darkness* it is already more complicated: the brigands, the speculators, the dishonest traders are easier to see, easier to understand, than the system which now, in the Congo—in the organised ivory market—begins to be apparent. It is a world of darkness of many kinds that this voyage explores, but among these kinds—the reminder is still critically necessary—is the reality of colonial exploitation, the ambiguity of the 'civilising mission' into Africa. As he put it to his publisher:

> the criminality of inefficiency and pure selfishness when tackling the civilising work in Africa.

But of course notice those terms: the mission is accepted, the criminality is a contingent failing. Much of the pressure of *Heart of Darkness* is in that uneasy relation. The colonial system is directly evoked; in the opening reference to the Romans (with its profound historical irony); then in the gunboat 'firing into a continent'; and above all in the contrasted scenes of the African chain-gang and the company clerk who to keep his books right has to shut out 'the groans of this sick person'.

> Each had an iron collar on his neck, and all were connected together with a chain whose bights swung between them, rhythmically clanking.
>
> ... The outraged law, like the bursting shells, had come to them, an insoluble mystery from the sea.
>
> He was devoted to his books which were in apple-pie order. Everything else in the station was in a muddle—heads, things, buildings.

'The criminality of inefficiency and pure selfishness.' But of course there is more than that.

> I've seen the devil of violence, and the devil of greed, and the devil of hot desire; but, by all the stars! These were strong, lusty, red-eyed devils, that swayed and drove men—men, I tell you. But as I stood on this hillside, I foresaw that in the blinding sunshine of that land I would become acquainted with a flabby, pretending, weak-eyed devil of a rapacious and pitiless folly. How insidious he could be, too, I was only to find out several months later and a thousand miles farther.

This transition is critical: the recognition of a new kind of devil.

And it is then astonishing that a whole school of criticism has succeeded in emptying *The Heart of Darkness* of its social and historical content, about which Conrad leaves us in no possible doubt. My quarrel with a whole tradition of criticism of fiction is about just this kind of endless reduction of deliberately created realities to analogues, symbolic circumstances, abstract situations. The Congo of Leopold follows the sea that Dombey and Son traded across, follows it into an endless substitution in which no object is itself, no social experience direct, but everything is translated into what can be called a metaphysical language—the river is Evil; the sea is Love or Death. Yet only called metaphysical, because there is not even that much guts in it. No profound and ordinary belief, only a perpetual and sophisticated evasion of these deliberately created, deliberately named, places and people, situations and experiences. It is an evasion masked by an imposed rhetoric—that playing with concepts of 'fiction' as alternatives to imaginatively written reality; concepts supported by discussions of technique which with all substance reduced or endlessly substituted can stand on their own as a detached methodology. It is then an abstract technique, playing with a series of abstract ideas; in the end a critic's fiction in which there is only method because the imaginative substance, the shaped reality of novels, is not available, is too much to conceive or to bear.

But of course you know the defence. The immediate situation, the local instance, is the Congo, but then what is developed is a 'larger' reality. And since all good novels depend on this kind of extension, so that they are more than the truth about only that man, that place, that time, this way of putting it can appear convincing. But there is all the difference in the world between discovering a general truth in a particular situation and making an abstract truth out of a contingent situation. It is the difference between creative seriousness and a now fashionable game.

Fashionable, I'd say, because what the 'truth' then is has its own content. Kurtz, we now learn, is an example of the veneer of civilised liberal humanist ideals; this pretence is stripped off to an essential savagery—'Exterminate all the brutes'. But what can be written in the 1950s to illustrate, in fantasy, that abstract and convenient conclusion (and then like *Lord of the Flies* is endlessly prescribed in school examinations, to teach attitudes that rationalise an arbitrary and conventional world) is as different as chalk and cheese from what happens in the Congo to Kurtz. He, the ivory-trader, up-river at the last station, is caught in the contradiction—(which is not just a structural irony but a lived and historical conflict) between the 'civilising work'—not humanism but the liberal rationale of imperialism —and the stress, the consequence of that 'rapacious and pitiless folly'. Conrad is at the full stretch of his powers in searching for and touching this heart of darkness. He sees it inevitably, first, as a matter of individual morality:

> there was something wanting in him—some small matter which, when the pressing need arose, could not be found under his magnificent eloquence.

But equally the flaw is revealed by a precise pressure:

the wilderness had found him out early, and had taken on him a terrible vengeance for the fantastic invasion.

And

> evidently the appetite for more ivory had got the better of the— what shall I say—less material aspirations.

An 'uncomplicated savagery'—the ordinary barbarism before the 'fantastic invasion'—is simpler and more acceptable than this 'lightless region of subtle horrors' in which the hollowness of the man finds an echo in the hollowness of the real pretension, the company's version of humanity:

> . . . the time was not ripe for vigorous action. Cautiously, cautiously—that's my principle. . . . Upon the whole the trade will suffer.

But what from a distance is calculation, the calculation of company policy, is under pressure a nightmare: 'the horror! the horror!', on 'that ivory face'.

These testing and breaking experiences, from Whalley to Kurtz, are Conrad's first extensions from the community of the ship, the temporarily isolated world of hard-lived common values. It is extremely important that he went on exploring quite away from the sea, but as we try to follow him we find we have to make some very difficult judgments.

Thus it is natural enough, given his base in experience, that in *The Secret Agent* he should offer to deal with what he sees as another destructive agency—anarchism. He sets it—or inserts it—in a familiar landscape: taking some hints from Dickens but more from the world he shared with Gissing and Wells:

> The vision of an enormous town presented itself, of a monstrous town more populous than some continents and in its man-made might as if indifferent to heaven's frowns and smiles; a cruel devourer of the world's light.

But now the lonely walker through the indifferent city is the anarchist with the bomb in his pocket. The reality of indifference is displaced, and the only centre of dependence is the Verloc family which the anarchist impulse—the imported impulse—destroys. Parts of *The Secret Agent* are very remarkable. Conrad uses his great powers in seeing betrayal, describing outrage and revenge. He projects these powers, most notably, into that one great scene, in which Winnie Verloc takes revenge for her brother by killing her husband. Projects: because the experience is in that way isolated; it is written as living sculpture, or we would now say as film:

> He was lying on his back and staring upwards. He saw partly on the ceiling and partly on the wall the moving shadow of an arm with a clenched hand holding a carving knife. It flickered up and down.

'Hazard has such accuracies': the sentence sticks in one's mind. For it isn't just a difference of political perspective—I don't like terrorism either, and I think at that point it was mad—that still makes one feel the whole concept is isolated in very damaging ways. Conrad's anarchists, for all the stage dressing—in and through the stage dressing—are sensational figures in a radically simplified world: a world abstracted like the ship—S.S. *London* moving through fog—right away from land, out of sight of the social system, the politics, the historical pressures and purposes which guide these hands, which have deformed and maddened so many hands, in acts of 'revenge', 'justice'—acts seen as revenge and as justice—but seen by Conrad, outside the closed community of the only visible unit the family, as only 'the moving shadow of an arm' flickering up and down: 'unbalanced nervous fury', unbalanced and senseless acts.

I can't feel in the end enough created reality past the impressive gestures of *The Secret Agent*. And I feel the same—more simply, because the work is more obviously diffuse—about *Under Western Eyes*. That narrative standing-off, which in other stories is a complexity of consciousness, is here again a gesture, the gesture of the title, offering to show us reality at the *end* of a process, with all its shaping forces assumed or referred to that fantastic 'Eastern' distance. Memories of Dostoievsky as before of Dickens, and the point reminds us that it isn't first a question of political sympathies—Dostoievsky in *The Devils* was more deeply hostile to what he was describing; more deeply because more intensely involved in it in a real country and among real ideas and feelings; not seeing it through the eyes of a teacher of languages at the exiles' end of the line.

It isn't at all there—in *The Secret Agent* or *Under Western Eyes* —that we find Conrad's genius in exploring that complicated community, that range of human actions and pressures, at which the simple community of the ship must eventually dock. Those are gestures from the top of his mind, gestures at two literatures which obliquely he had to come to some sort of terms with: English and Russian, those radically different but lived, settled, autonomously disturbing experiences. He makes his own identity most completely, his identity as a novelist, when he imagines and creates from his whole experience: an experience he could render just because he was not in those national ways rooted; not settled, not limited and preoccupied as those national novelists were bound to be; but able to move, to observe, where countries, systems, values interact; where this is itself the action and the society: the action and society of *Nostromo*.

It we look back from *Nostromo* to the early sea stories we can gather this essential change. There is a moment when Nostromo and Decoud are taking the company's silver away in a boat to prevent it falling into the hands of the approaching revolutionary army. They are almost sunk by Sotillo's steamer: two men in the lighter, in a common physical danger. But then listen:

Decoud pumped without intermission. Nostromo steered without relaxing for a second the intense, peering effort of his stare. Each of them was as if utterly alone with his task. It did not occur to them to speak. There was nothing in common between them but the knowledge that the damaged lighter must be slowly but surely sinking. In that knowledge, which was like the crucial test of their desires, they seemed to have become completely estranged, as if they had discovered in the very shock of the collision that the loss of the silver would not mean the same thing to them both. This common danger brought their differences in aim, in view, in character, and in position, into absolute prominence in the private vision of each. There was no bond of conviction, of common idea; they were merely two adventurers pursuing each his own adventure, involved in the same imminence of deadly peril. Therefore they had nothing to say to each other.

'Nothing in common between them'; 'no bond of conviction, of common idea': this is the new experience, the new social experience, which complicates and surpasses the simple and customary virtues. Isolation, now, is a new and varying quality. The 'sane materialism' of Decoud dissolves:

Solitude from mere outward condition of existence becomes very swiftly a state of soul in which the affectations of irony and scepticism have no place. It takes possession of the mind, and drives forth the thought into the exile of utter unbelief. After three days of waiting for the sight of some human face, Decoud caught himself entertaining a doubt of his own individuality. It had merged into the world of cloud and water, of natural forces and forms of nature. In our activity alone do we find the sustaining illusion of an independent existence as against the whole scheme of things of which we form a helpless part.

And I remember, hearing that, the voice of Captain MacWhirr: 'facing it—always facing it—that's the way to get through'. What has happened is the disappearance of a *social* value. It is this disappearance that is learned, tragically learned, by Nostromo, by 'our man', the trading company's man, the faithful servant of the traders. Taking the mining company's silver away, Decoud tells him:

> 'You were the man for the task.'
>
> 'I was, but I cannot believe,' said Nostromo, 'that its loss would have impoverished Don Carlos Gould very much. There is more wealth in the mountain. I have heard it rolling down the shoots on quiet nights. . . . For years the rich rocks have been pouring down with a noise like thunder, and the miners say that there is enough at the heart of the mountain to thunder on for years and years to come. And yet, the day before yesterday, we have been fighting to save it from the mob, and tonight I am sent out with it into this darkness . . . as if it were the last lot of silver on earth to get bread for the hungry with. . . . Well, I am going to make it the most famous and desperate affair of my life.'

These now are the questions: not the strength and devotion of the trusted servant but in the clash of real interests a revaluation:

> Nostromo interrupted his reflections upon the way men's qualities are made use of . . .

Made use of by what?

> 'There is no peace and no rest in the development of material interests. They have their law and their justice. But it is founded on expediency, and is inhuman; it is without rectitude, without the continuity and the force that can be found only in a moral principle. Mrs Gould, the time approaches when all that the Gould Concession stands for shall weigh as heavily upon the people as the barbarian cruelty and misrule of a few years back.'

That's Monyghan the doctor near the end of the novel. And what he says directly the whole world of the novel enforces.

From the decade of Katanga the politics of Sulaco are not difficult to understand.

> Justly incensed at the grinding oppression of foreigners, actuated by sordid motives of gain rather than by love for a country where they come impoverished to seek their fortunes. . . .
>
> . . . The mine, which by every law, international, human, and divine, reverts now to the Government as national property. . . .

That is the rhetoric, the consolidating rhetoric, of the first
revolt of the miners. But the new government misses the
income, and later invites Gould in on a perpetual concession of
which the condition is an advance of royalties. The whole
politics of the province are determined in these ways by the
wealth of the mine:

> double-edged with the cupidity and misery of mankind, steeped
> in all the voices of self-indulgence as in a concoction of poisonous
> roots, tainting the very cause for which it is drawn, always ready
> to turn awkwardly in the hand.

That is the sad wisdom of Gould himself: an old and tired
imperialism. The recognition is followed, directly, by the
desperate, disillusioned resolve:

> There was nothing for it, now, but to go on using it.

Meanwhile 'the considerable personage' of San Francisco is
waiting:

> There's no hurry. Time itself has got to wait on the greatest
> country in the whole of God's universe. We shall be giving the
> word for everything: industry, trade, law, journalism, art,
> politics and religion, from Cape Horn clear over to Smith's
> Sound, and beyond, too, if anything worth taking hold of turns
> up at the North Pole. And then we shall have the leisure to take
> in hand the outlying islands and continents of the earth. We shall
> run the world's business whether the world likes it or not.

Gould, ironically, has 'no objection to this theory of the
world's future'. But caught in the local political consequences
he fights

> in the defence of the commonest decencies of organised society.

That is the world, the clash of interests and of cultures, in
which Nostromo has been accustomed to serve. It goes its way;
Conrad has no illusions about it or about its future. After the
revolt and the new Constitution

it was like a second youth, like a new life, full of promise, of unrest, of toil, scattering lavishly its wealth to the four corners of an excited world. National changes swept along in the train of material interests. And other changes more subtle, outwardly unmarked, affected the minds and hearts of the workers.

Monyghan becomes the medical officer of San Tomé Consolidated Mines and Inspector-General of State Hospitals. But for Conrad, for the man of virtue, the decisive history is the history of Nostromo.

What happens to his capacity for strength and loyalty? Disconnected, isolated, the servant of interests he no longer respects but cut off from others in the very act of serving, he has no self to speak of, no identity and no future but the hidden silver. And yet for him in the end this is nothing, because there is no order, no society, in which he can set it to work. There is a brief vanity but also the consciousness of the wealth that is taken from the hands of the poor. Nostromo dies in error, in isolation and error. He makes no answer to the organiser who wants the silver to fight capitalism. He offers the silver back where it had once belonged, with the Goulds, but Mrs Gould, disturbed by the trouble of keeping it, hates 'the idea of that silver from the bottom of my heart'. Nostromo is shot, in error, by the old revolutionary, the nineteenth-century figure, the old hero who fought simply for national liberty. All that is left, and it seems everything, is the love that Nostromo gave and inspired: the love and strength of a man, 'a man of the people', who is destroyed by the complexity of the action around him, the clash of interests and cultures.

And it is when we see that—that end of 'the magnificent Capataz de Cargadores', of Fidanza, of 'son Gian' Battista, of Nostromo—that end of a complex of strengths and relationships: when we reflect on that we have found our way through the complex meanings of isolation. What we see there, strongly, is not isolation the condition, the condition of man; but isolation the *response*, the tragic response, to an action and a history that has changed and still changes: extending, connecting beyond customary meanings and beyond national frontiers: the unique, the deliberately created, the imagined and now known world of that Polish Englishman: the unsettled and exploring, sea-crossing Conrad.

VII

Alone in the City

IN the second half of the nineteenth century most English
experience was urban but most English fiction was rural. It
is significant and puzzling that after the genius of Dickens the
creative development of the English novel, for a full generation,
was in George Eliot and Hardy a matter of rural and small-
town experience. It seems to me probable that the urban popular
culture, which was continuing to extend, was losing in this
period its creative potential. In the period of high imperialism
especially it is increasingly visible as a false consciousness; a self-
enclosed and subordinate alternative culture. This is perhaps
even more evident when we see how its radical element
developed and separated out as a conscious political position.

There is one significantly isolated case in the early years of
the new century, in just these terms: Robert Tressell's *Ragged-
Trousered Philanthropists*. This must be related to Dickens.
Tressell sees his town as Mugsborough; his characters as
Sweater, Hunter and Slyme. But there are also the neutral
workers, and the new figures—Owen, Barrington—of the conscious socialists. Yet Tressell's strength is not in the conscious
exposition (its problems of identity and relationship are in fact
unresolved). His strength is in the anonymous, collective,
popular idiom through which a working world is strongly,
closely, ironically seen. What is then interesting is that despite
this vigour the final judgment is ironical: the ragged-trousered
philanthropists—those who in the end accept exploitation; the
inhabitants of Mugsborough. It is a generous irony, from within
the working class, and as such humane. That it was published

only by chance, and then in a doctored form—now known and replaced by the original—is entirely consistent with the general history.

The more immediate tradition, following Dickens, is that of Gissing and Wells. In Gissing especially there are some significant changes. He has absorbed the methods of the realist writers, as in *Demos* and *The Nether World*. He belongs also with George Eliot and Hardy, for all his differences of tone, in an acute awareness of the problems of the separated individual and of education as a function of separation. *Born in Exile* and *The Unclassed* are important novels of this kind. And what is then interesting is the way this experience of separation—the consciousness of the educated observer—relates to the major experience of the city.

> The canal—*maladetta e sventurata fossa*—stagnating in utter foulness between coal-wharfs and builders' yards, at this point divides two neighbourhoods of different aspects. On the south is Hoxton, a region of malodorous market streets, of factories, timber-yards, grimy warehouses, of alleys swarming with small trades and crafts, of filthy courts and passages leading into pestilential gloom; everywhere toil in its most degrading forms; the thoroughfares thundering with high-laden waggons, the pavements trodden by working folk of the coarsest type, the corners and lurking-holes showing destitution at its ugliest. Walking northwards, the explorer finds himself in freer air, amid broader ways, in a district of dwelling houses only; the roads seem abandoned to milkmen, cat's-meat vendors, and costermongers. Here will be found streets in which every window has its card advertising lodgings; others claim a higher respectability, the houses retreating behind patches of garden-ground, and occasionally showing plastered pillars and a balcony. The change is from undisguised struggle for subsistence to mean and spirit-broken leisure; hither retreat the better-paid of the great slave-army when they are free to eat and sleep. To walk about a neighbourhood such as this is the dreariest exercise to which man

can betake himself; the heart is crushed by uniformity of decent squalor; one remembers that each of these dead-faced houses, often each separate blind window, represents a 'home', and the associations of the word whisper blank despair.

'To walk about a neighbourhood such as this'; 'the canal—*maladetta e sventurata fossa*'; this consciousness is not difficult to identify. And it is important how often a critical experience of the city has been expressed in this way: the man walking and watching in the streets. It is as early as Blake:

> *I wander thro' each charter'd street*
> *Near where the charter'd Thames does flow,*
> *And mark in every face I meet,*
> *Marks of weakness, marks of woe.*

And then, as I said earlier, Wordsworth, in that great seventh book of *The Prelude*—'Residence in London':

> *O Friend! one feeling was there which belong'd*
> *To this great City, by exclusive right.*
> *How often in the overflowing Streets,*
> *Have I gone forward with the Crowd, and said*
> *Unto myself, the face of everyone*
> *That passes by me is a mystery.*
> *Thus have I look'd, nor ceas'd to look, oppress'd*
> *By thoughts of what, and whither, when and how*
> *Until the shapes before my eyes became*
> *A second-sight procession, such as glides*
> *Over still mountains, or appears in dreams;*
> *And all the ballast of familiar life,*
> *The present, and the past; hope, fear; all stays,*
> *All laws of acting, thinking, speaking man*
> *Went from me, neither knowing me, nor known.*

In the universe of strangers, as the city can be taken to be, social identity—'all laws of acting, thinking, speaking man'—can seem to be lost. There are then two obvious responses. There is the conversion of people seen in this way to a crowd, to masses:

> *Oh, blank confusion! and a type not false*
> *Of what the mighty City is itself*
> *To all except a Straggler here and there,*
> *To the whole Swarm of its inhabitants;*
> *An undistinguishable world to men,*
> *The slaves unrespited of low pursuits,*
> *Living amid the same perpetual flow*
> *Of trivial objects, melted and reduced*
> *To one identity, by differences*
> *That have no law, no meaning, and no end.*

Or later in Hardy (but not in his fiction):

As the crowd grows denser it loses its character of an aggregate of countless units, and becomes an organic whole, a molluscous black creature having nothing in common with humanity, that takes the shapes of the streets along which it has lain itself, and throws out horrid excrescences and limbs into neighbouring alleys; a creature whose voice exudes from its scaly coat, and who has an eye in every pore of its body. The balconies, stands and railway-bridge are occupied by small detached shapes of the same tissue, but of gentler motion, as if they were the spawn of the monster in the midst.

This way of seeing has deeply influenced modern literature in many imaginative forms, and it's difficult to disentangle it from a more convincing observation, as again in Hardy:

London appears not to *see itself*. Each individual is conscious of *himself*, but nobody conscious of themselves collectively, except perhaps some poor gaper who stares round with a half-idiotic aspect.

And this poor gaper, half-idiotic, is we suppose inevitably up from the country.

But that is the isolated observer, the man speaking in his own voice. In the novel during the nineteenth century it is an unfamiliar response. The commitment to characters makes its method uneasy. We have seen the variety of Dickens's response: the dramatisation of very similar feelings—the monster, the indifferent stream—but also, through the commitment to characters, the necessary recognitions which the crowd as such may prevent, may be designed to prevent. The experience was again dramatised by Elizabeth Gaskell, in *Mary Barton*:

> It is a pretty sight to walk through a street with lighted shops; the gas is so brilliant, the display of goods so much more vividly shown than by day, and of all shops the druggist's looks the most like the tales of our childhood, from Aladdin's garden of enchanted fruits to the charming Rosamund with her purple jar.
>
> No such associations had Barton; yet he felt the contrast between the well-filled, well-lighted shops and the dim gloomy cellar, and it made him moody that such contrasts should exist. They are the mysterious problem of life to more than him. He wondered if any in all the hurrying crowd had come from such a house of mourning. He thought they all looked joyous, and he was angry with them. But he could not, you cannot, read the lot of those who daily pass you by in the street. How do you know the wild romances of their lives; the trials, the temptations they are even now enduring, resisting, sinking under? You may be elbowed one instant by the girl desperate in her abandonment, laughing in mad merriment with her outward gesture, while her soul is longing for the rest of the dead, and bringing itself to think of the cold-flowing river as the only mercy of God remaining to her here. You may pass the criminal, meditating crimes at which you will tomorrow shudder with horror as you read them. You may push against one, humble and unnoticed, the last upon earth, who in Heaven will for ever be in the immediate light of God's countenance. Errands of mercy—errands of sin—did you ever think where all the thousands of people you daily meet are bound?

What is interesting here is the humanity of the response. The instances perhaps are naive and generalised, but they are offered as a way of understanding and sympathising. It is the mood of Dickens though less complex and less dramatic: an insistence

on human recognition just because the obstacles, the contradictions, are so clearly seen.

That is the second response: not the image of the crowd
which then acts in its own terms, but the recognition of a social
experience which the writer must penetrate. Gissing is important because these very different responses are almost equally
strong in his work. He is the humane observer describing the
urban landscape and its social experience, trying to individualise
beyond it. He is also the man who enacts in himself the alienation he is witnessing; who sees in the despair of others not only
his own despair but the shapes of recoil: the drawing back, do-
not-touch-me kind of exile.

Gissing wrote about Dickens in ways that show the connection and the change, and he returned again and again to the
image of London:

> London as a place of squalid mystery and terror, of the grimly
> grotesque, of labyrinthine obscurity and lurid fascination, is
> Dickens's own; he taught English people a certain way of
> regarding the huge city and to this day how common it is to see
> London with Dickens's eyes. . . .
>
> . . . a great gloomy city, webbed and meshed, as it were, by the
> spinnings of a huge poisonous spider. . . .
>
> . . . murky, swarming, rotting London, a marvellous rendering
> of the impression received by any imaginative person who, in
> low spirits, has had occasion to wander about London's streets.

'An imaginative person in low spirits': the characterisation of
Gissing himself seems almost too apt. What has gone from the
Dickens vision is the energy of sympathy, the delighted sharing
of experience. Gissing was right when he described Dickens as
opening 'the new era of democracy in letters', but his own
difficulty is indicated in his immediate qualification:

> The sure test of vulgarity is that it debases whatever it takes note
> of. Dickens on the other hand cannot touch the commonest

coarsest detail of ignoble life but at once it gains a certain suggestiveness.

That's not how it was. 'The commonest coarsest detail of ignoble life': that is never Dickens, before or after touching; it is the new language, the anxious language, of the recoil.

Recoil, certainly, includes indignation:

It was the hour of the unyoking of men. In the highways and byways of Clerkenwell there was a thronging of released toilers, of young and old, of male and female. Forth they streamed from factories and workrooms, anxious to make the most of the few hours during which they might live for themselves. Great numbers were still bent over their labour, and would be for hours to come, but the majority had leave to wend stablewards. Along the main thoroughfares the wheel-track was clangorous; every omnibus that clattered by was heavily laden with passengers; tarpaulins gleamed over the knees of those who sat outside. This way and that the lights were blurred into a misty radiance; overhead was mere blackness, whence descended the lashing rain. There was a ceaseless scattering of mud; there were blocks in the traffic, attended with rough jest or angry curse; there was jostling on the crowded pavement. Public-houses began to brighten up, to bestir themselves for the evening's business. Streets that had been hives of activity since early morning were being abandoned to silence and darkness and the sweeping wind.

That is a bitter landscape, bitterly and indignantly observed: the highways and byways of a social system. But Gissing hardly ever connects with it. He sees it, as narrator or through his characters, in recoil:

What terrible barracks, those Farringdon Road Buildings! Vast, sheer walls, unbroken by even an attempt at ornament; row above row of windows in the mud-coloured surface, upwards, upwards, lifeless eyes, mirky openings that tell of bareness, disorder, comfortlessness within. One is tempted to say that Shooter's Gardens are a preferable abode. An inner courtyard, asphalted, swept clean,—looking up to the sky as from a prison.

Acres of these edifices, the tinge of grime declaring the relative dates of their erection; millions of tons of brute brick and mortar, crushing the spirit as you gaze. Barracks, in truth; housing for the army of industrialism, an army fighting with itself, rank against rank, man against man, that the survivors may have whereon to feed. Pass by in the night, and strain imagination to picture the weltering mass of human weariness, of bestiality, of unmerited dolour, of hopeless hope, of crushed surrender, tumbled together within those forbidding walls.

Clara hated the place from her first hour in it. It seemed to her that the air was poisoned with the odour of an unclean crowd. The yells of children at play in the courtyard tortured her nerves; the regular sounds on the staircase, day after day repeated at the same hours, incidents of the life of poverty, irritated her sick brain and filled her with despair to think that as long as she lived she could never hope to rise again above this world to which she was born.

That is the authentic and powerful note of Gissing: the indignation and despair, but also the ragged nerves, the whine, of the separated frustrated life-carrying individual, not only aware of but against 'the weltering mass'. It is almost contemporary with *Tess* and *Jude* but the sound of the voice could hardly be more different.

That is why Wells, I suppose, moving around a more comfortable London came as a positive relief: a recovery of energy. It's not, I've already said, the energy of Dickens, though Wells obviously learned from him. It's smaller, chirpier; not so much energy as bounce. Yet it gains a perspective by its dimension of social comparison: that conviction so widely shared at the turn of the century that renewal was possible, if we could only see and understand the outdated social system which both oppressed and confused. Wells's confidence comes from his conviction that what is wrong can be explained and understood. This is the mood of his description in *Tono Bungay* of a wedding in the city:

162

Under stress of tradition we were all of us trying in the fermenting chaos of London to carry out the marriage ceremonies of a Bladesover tenant or one of the chubby middling sort of people in some dependent country town. There a marriage is a public function with a public significance. There the church is to a large extent the gathering-place of the community, and your going to be married a thing of importance to everyone you pass on the road. It is a change of status that quite legitimately interests the whole neighbourhood. But in London there are no neighbours, nobody knows, nobody cares. An absolute stranger in an office took my notice, and our banns were proclaimed to ears that had never previously heard our names. The clergyman, even, who married us had never seen us before, and didn't in any degree intimate that he wanted to see us again.

Neighbours in London! The Ramboats did not know the names of the people on either side of them. As I waited for Marion before we started off upon our honeymoon flight, Mr Ramboat, I remember, came and stood beside me and stared out of the window.

'There was a funeral over there yestiday,' he said by way of making conversation, and moved his head at the house opposite. 'Quite a smart affair it was—with a glass 'earse. . . .'

. . . Our little procession of three carriages with white-favour-adorned horses and drivers, went through all the huge, noisy, indifferent traffic like a lost china image in the coal-chute of an ironclad. Nobody made way for us, nobody cared for us; the driver of an omnibus jeered; for a long time we crawled behind an unamiable dustcart.

The irrelevant clatter and tumult gave a queer flavour of indecency to this public coming-together of lovers. We seemed to have obtruded ourselves shamelessly. The crowd that gathered outside the church would have gathered in the same spirit and with greater alacrity for a street accident. . . .

This is sober even grim as it describes indifference, but a confident laugh, a retrospective laugh seems to be waiting just beyond it, as the details are rehearsed. And 'fermenting chaos'; 'a weltering mass': those are of course the difference between Wells and Gissing. But there is also something else, as we look forward from Wells to the changes in the novel that in a way bypassed him, went in quite other directions. Just as his description of the city wedding depends on available comparisons with a wedding in the country or in a small town, so his confident explanatory stance, the stance of the observer, depends on a particular certainty. It depends on the omniscience of the novelist. That is to say on an effective convention between writer and reader that what is commonly seen can be commonly understood.

It is this convention that in a new generation was to be dramatically broken. A new imaginative stance had been already deeply prepared. This was not the confident looker-on, the explaining observer, but the man alone in the street, as far back in Wordsworth, who feels not only the mystery, the impenetrability, of those who go past him but who in this repeated uncertainty loses his own familiar bearings, his own sense of identity, his own capacity to communicate:

> *All laws of acting, thinking, speaking man*
> *Went from me, neither knowing me, nor known.*

It is from this disturbance, essentially, that much modern fiction—and especially modern urban fiction—has been written. The laws and the conventions of traditional observation and communication have seemed to disappear. The consequent awareness is intense and fragmentary, subjective only, yet in the very form of its subjectivity including others who are now with the buildings, the noises, the sights and smells of the city parts of this single and racing consciousness. The great novel of the modern city in this way of seeing is of course Joyce's *Ulysses*. We can listen to just this experience as Bloom walks through Dublin:

> He crossed to the bright side, avoiding the loose cellarflap of
> number seventy-five. The sun was nearing the steeple of George's

church. Be a warm day I fancy. Specially in these black clothes
feel it more. Black conducts, reflects (refracts is it?) the heat. But
I couldn't go in that light suit. Make a picnic of it. His eyelids
sank quietly often as he walked in happy warmth. Boland's
breadvan delivering with trays our daily but she prefers yester-
day's loaves turnovers crisp crowns hot. Makes you feel young.
Somewhere in the east: early morning: set off at dawn, travel
round in front of the sun, steal a day's march on him. Keep it up for
ever never grow a day older technically. Walk along a strand,
strange land, come to a city gate, sentry there, old ranker too, old
Tweedy's big moustaches leaning on a long kind of a spear.
Wander through awned streets. Turbaned faces going by. Dark
caves of carpet shops, big man, Turko the terrible, seated cross-
legged smoking a coiled pipe. Cries of sellers in the streets. Drink
water scented with fennel, sherbet. Wander along all day. Might
meet a robber or two. Well, meet him. Getting on to sundown.
The shadows of the mosques along the pillars: priest with a
scroll rolled up. A shiver of the trees, signal, the evening wind.
I pass on. Fading gold sky. A mother watches from her door-
way. She calls her children home in their dark language. High
wall: beyond strings twanged. Night sky moon, violet, colour
of Molly's new garters. Strings. Listen. A girl playing one of
these instruments what do you call them: dulcimers. I pass.

Here the fantasy of the Oriental city begins from the smell
of bread in Boland's van, but each sight or sound or smell is a
trigger to Bloom's private preoccupations. Under the pressure
of his needs, the one city as it passes is as real as the other. This
is the profound alteration. The forces of the action have become
internal and in a way there is no longer a city, there is only a
man walking through it. Elizabeth Gaskell, we remember, went
from the window of the druggists to 'Aladdin's garden of en-
chanted fruits', but within a rigidly controlled objective frame:
'the tales of our childhood'—writer and reader can share this
memory; 'no such associations had Barton'—the objectively
seen character, separate in situation and in culture, is made
sharply distinct. In *Ulysses* the relation between action and

consciousness, but also the relation between narrator and character, has been modulated until the whole shape of the language has changed:

> He approached Larry O'Rourke's. From the cellar grating floated up the flabby gush of porter. Through the open doorway the bar squirted out sniffs of ginger, teadust, biscuitmush. Good house, however: just the end of the city traffic. For instance McAuley's down there: n.g. as position. Of course if they ran a tramline along the North Circular from the cattle market to the quays value would go up like a shot.
>
> Bald head over the blind. Cute old codger. No use canvassing him for an ad. Still he knows his own business best. There he is, sure enough, my bold Larry, leaning against the sugarbin in his shirtsleeves watching the aproned curate swab up with mop and bucket. Simon Dedalus takes him off to a tee with his eyes screwed up. Do you know what I'm going to tell you? What's that Mr O'Rourke? Do you know what? The Russians, they'd only be an eight o'clock breakfast for the Japanese.
>
> Stop and say a word: about the funeral perhaps. Sad thing about poor Dignam, Mr O'Rourke.
>
> Turning into Dorset Street he said freshly in greeting through the doorway:
>
> —Good day Mr O'Rourke
> —Good day to you
> —Lovely weather, sir
> —'Tis all that

Here the contrast of dimensions is direct: the substance of Bloom's observations, speculations, memories—on a thread of narrative action—is an active exchange, even an active community, within the imagined speech of thought, while what is actually said when he reaches O'Rourke is flat and external: what the received conventions have become. The substantial reality, the living variety of the city is in the walker's mind:

> He walked along the curbstone. Stream of life. . . .
> . . . Cityful passing away, other cityful coming, passing away too: other coming on, passing on. Houses, lines of houses, streets,

miles of pavements, piledup bricks, stones. Changing hands. This
owner, that. Landlord never dies they say. Other steps into his
shoes when he gets his notice to quit. They buy the place up with
gold and still they have all the gold. Swindle in it somewhere.
Piled up in cities, worn away age after age. Pyramids in sand.
Built on bread and onions. Slaves. Chinese wall. Babylon. Big
Stones left. Round towers. Rest rubble, sprawling suburbs,
jerrybuilt, Kerwan's mushroom houses, built of breeze. Shelter
for the night.

No one is anything.

Joyce's originality in these parts of his work is remarkable. It is
a necessary innovation if this way of seeing—fragmentary,
miscellaneous, isolated—is to be actualised on the senses in a
new structure of language. The genius of *Ulysses* is that it
dramatises three minds—Bloom, Stephen and Molly—and their
interaction is the necessary tension. But what each enacts for the
other is a symbolic role, and the reality to which they must
ultimately relate is no longer a place and a time, for all the
anxious dating of that day in Dublin. It is an abstracted or more
strictly an imposed pattern of man and woman, father and son;
a family but not a family, out of touch and searching for each
other through a myth and a history. The history is not in this
city but in the loss of a city, the loss of relationships. The only
knowable community is in the need, the desire, of a racing
separated consciousness.

But what must also be said, as we see this new structure, is
that the most deeply known human community is language
itself. And it is a paradox that in *Ulysses*, through its patterns of
loss and frustration, there is not only search but discovery: of
an ordinary language, heard more clearly than anywhere in the
realist novel before it; a positive flow of that wider human
speech which has been screened and strained by the prevailing
social conventions: conventions of separation, reduction, in the
actual history. The greatness of *Ulysses* is this community of

speech. That is its difference from *Finnegans Wake* in which a single voice—a voice offering to speak for everyone and everything, 'Here Comes Everybody'—carries the dissolution to a change of quality in which the strains already evident in the later sections of *Ulysses* (before the last monologue) have increased so greatly that the interchange of voices—public and private, the voices of a city heard and overheard—has given way to a surrogate, a universal isolated language. Where *Ulysses* was the climax *Finnegans Wake* is the crisis of the development we have been tracing: of the novel and community; the novel and the city; the novel of 'acting, thinking, speaking' man.

VIII

D. H. Lawrence

IT is often the case that we read writers backwards: from the finished work, the mature achievements, to the early work, the beginnings. Certainly this can show a pattern of significant development, but of course the critical finding is there from the start in the procedure adopted. We read the early works for signs of how the later ones came to be written. And this can leave out, obviously, other possible findings, such as failures to develop some particular early quality. But when we are looking at the way the novel has developed, in certain gifted hands and under specific pressures, these points about development—negative as well as positive—may be of the greatest importance.

Lawrence, I think, has suffered from being read backwards: from what is seen as the internationally significant work between *Women in Love* and *Lady Chatterley's Lover* to what can be seen as the provincial beginnings in *Sons and Lovers* and the early stories. If this were only a contrast between provincial and international it need not detain us; that kind of growth would indeed be significant. But as always in these phrases a value judgment is there and is concealed. Lawrence's themes and methods in his later work can be presented in such a way that they are only achievement: a necessarily more significant structure of feeling. What he lost along the way—what I think he knew he had lost and struggled to recover—may in fact be just as important as what he undoubtedly gained. This is especially relevant if we have learned too well a very common definition of what is 'early' and what is 'mature' Lawrence: one which excludes *Lady Chatterley's Lover* as a late and misguided work, and includes only the development from *Sons and Lovers* through *The Rainbow* to *Women in Love*. The real development I believe is much more complicated than that. It is a series of advances and deadlocks, and then renewed advance; and at each stage, both because Lawrence was the most gifted English novelist of his time and because for many reasons his problems were central to a main current of growth and difficulty in our society and our culture, his decisions and their consequences— the achievements and the limitations—are of quite exceptional importance.

I read Lawrence of course as an English novelist. I don't mean that he didn't learn some important things from writers outside English, as so many of his predecessors had been learning. The novel had been crossing frontiers to everyone's advantage for more than a century. But to most writers the work in their own language has a special importance, and it is then not only significant but quite unsurprising that at a very critical stage of his development, in 1914, he should write his *Study of Thomas Hardy*. This is as he said about everything but Hardy—actually that's an exaggeration; it includes some very detailed and direct response to the older novelist—but then it's significant that Lawrence, in effect deciding the future direction of his life, should try to get his thoughts and feelings clear in relation and in response to the writer who is obviously (if we can look without prejudice) his direct and most important English predecessor. To go from *The Woodlanders* and *Tess* and *Jude* to *The Rainbow* and *Women in Love* and *Lady Chatterley's Lover* is to know this, directly, in feeling. That Hardy and Lawrence are eventually very different is clear enough, but that they started, at different times, from very closely related situations feelings and ideas—from a landscape, a country, a society, a people, a working community; from connected desires and the frustration of desires—is in my view just as clear. And what a novelist is learning in feelings and ideas—often learning by criticising, by altering, by rejecting—he learns perhaps most closely in his language, his organisation of language; in the substance of the novel itself.

I have referred already to that significant grouping of George Eliot, Hardy and Lawrence as 'our three great autodidacts'. And the way I see this most directly is in the problem of language: in the extension of practical community which their life-experience gave them; in the inclusion in their novels of people hitherto unwritten about, or at best observed from a distance; in the new and critical experience of craftsmen, artisans, labourers, miners. What I've stressed as the problem in this—and it is a continuing problem—is the relation between the language of the novelist—always in some measure an educated language, as it has to be if the full account is to be given, and the language of these newly described men and women— a familiar language, steeped in a place and in work; often different in profound as well as in simple ways—and to the novelist consciously different—from the habits of education: the class, the method, the underlying sensibility. It isn't only a matter of relating disparate idioms, though that technically is how it often appears. It is basically a matter of living relationships; of our actual connections with others and with elements of ourselves.

Belonging and not belonging: that is the crisis through all these writers. A deprived and frustrating way of life in which, all the same, loving, listening, sharing, remembering, we have been raised; a way which we hear in our mouths, feel in our bodies, interacting (that makes it sound comfortable) with other ways, other feelings, other languages we have heard. I think of the importance for Lawrence of what were really other languages—French, German, Italian, Spanish; what he had learned

in education; another way through, way out of, an impoverished but still native speech; other ways of living, eventually,
that he could go and try to share. It was always simpler, for
good reasons, to go to these other real languages—at least to
make certain things clearer—than along the metalled road to
what was only but was audibly, emphatically, the language of
another class. 'How beastly the bourgeois is.' But that was later,
when he had got away from it; when he could let his full anger
out. In the beginning it was harder; harder I mean than abuse,
which discharges the difficulty but can't make it clearer where
it matters.

I have been talking of difficulty but when I read Lawrence's
early work—especially the stories up to *Odour of Chrysanthemums*, the first three plays, and then *Sons and Lovers*—what I
really find is a sort of miracle of language. In those early years
before the other difficulties started—difficulties he had to go on
to—what he achieved is marvellous, by any standard at all. The
language and the feeling—new language, new feelings—come
alive together. What really comes alive is community, and
when I say community I mean something which is of course
personal: a man feeling with others, speaking in and with them.
I'm thinking of *White Stocking*, of *Goose Fair*, of *A Sick Collier*
and *Second Best*. Or here, for we need to listen to it, in *Odour of
Chrysanthemums*:

> . . . She heard the engine move slowly, and the brakes made
> no sound. The old woman did not notice. Elizabeth waited
> in suspense. The mother-in-law talked, with lapses into
> silence.
> 'But he wasn't your son, Lizzie, an' it makes a difference.
> Whatever he was, I remember him when he was little, an' I
> learned to understand him and to make allowances. You've got
> to make allowances for them—'
> It was half-past ten, and the old woman was saying: 'But it's
> trouble from beginning to end; you're never too old for trouble,

never too old for that—' when the gate banged back, and there
were heavy feet on the steps.

'I'll go, Lizzie, let me go,' cried the old woman, rising. But
Elizabeth was at the door. It was a man in pit-clothes.

'They're bringing 'im, Missis,' he said.

If I make about that a merely technical point, it's only as a way
of getting through to the feeling: the underlying feeling that is
more than just the situation: the dead miner, the dead son and
husband being carried home. What is new here, really new, is
that the language of the writer is at one with the language of his
characters, in a way that hadn't happened, though George Eliot
and Hardy had tried, since the earlier smaller community of the
novel had been extended and changed. That sentence beginning 'It was half-past ten', for example, includes what the old
woman says and what the writer has also to tell us in an unbroken sequence; when her words trail off—'never too old for
that' then 'the gate banged back': we are in the same world, the
same language.

It is easy to say that any gifted writer could do this. Actually
since Lawrence made this change—altering the novelist's language of description and analysis to the colloquial and informal
from the abstract and polite—many writers have followed him;
we have even got used to it. But of course the real change isn't
technical at all. He is writing like that because he is feeling with
his people, not of them or about them, but within a particular
flow—what he once called sympathy but it isn't that formal;
he is simply writing where he lived, and paradoxically—when
we look at the difficulty of the history—with an art all the more
impressive because when it succeeds it seems given.

And it is in just this sense—this particular sense—that I read
Sons and Lovers. Of course it is true that within this flow, this
essential community, what is experienced again and again is
not only closeness and sympathy but conflict, loss, frustration

and despair. It's no part of any intelligent case about the reality of community that its experiences are only positive. On the contrary, as in this specific case, these are people pressed by poverty, by breaking physical work, by overcrowding and then by all the resentments confusions misunderstandings that follow. Also of course people are relating directly, in love and marriage, or as parents and children, through all the ordinary difficulties of any relationship and growth.

Now this early Lawrence novel can be assimilated to the later work because it expresses, centrally, a general theme: a tied relation between mother and son and the consequent difficulty of loving relations with others: something that can be abstracted and even made theoretical and that in any case happens in families and communities of very many kinds. In a simple way the assimilation is fair but what it masks is a quite crucial problem in Lawrence's later fiction: the degree to which such a primary relationship—I mean of course our understanding of it through fiction; the way, with the novelist, we see and value it—can be affected by being isolated from a wider and continuing life, to say nothing of being abstracted in a more conscious way, or of being as it were theoretically composed.

As a matter of reading, anyway, I don't think we can just lift the single experience out. That it is happening there in that family, in that general life, is how Lawrence wrote it and how we have to respond to it. And this is more than just saying that as well as the primary relationship we also get what people call a portrait of a mining family, a mining community. That isn't there as an extra. It's part of the experience. The mother's offer to her son, part of her real offer—which of course is not only of herself as a woman or even of herself as a mother—is very specific to that life. It isn't only an offer of a kind of love, a kind of sex or delay of sex; it's of a whole way of growing up—the deliberate contrast with the father who is there in his pit-clothes and his drinking; an alternative then, a conscious alternative to her own sense of waste, of degradation even; a projected idea of what a good life would be, what getting on would be—as Clym's mother had put it in *The Return of the Native*. It's a physical primary relationship between mother and son, between a mother and her sons, and it is lived through in many ways: in the contrast between the mother and Miriam; between the miner and the tidy young clerk; between the Bottoms and Haggs Farm. Lived through that is to say as a whole and continuing experience, in which what can easily be separated as personal and social are in fact, in a life, known as a single complicated process. And Lawrence writes of this with a closeness and a continuity that are still unsurpassed; writing *with* the experience; with the mother as well as the son; with the life they belong to that is more, much more than a portrait or an environment or a background. That is why I still think it is a very great novel, and I emphasise the achievement as indeed that; not a preliminary, an achievement.

Where then does the difficulty start? In *Sons and Lovers*, it seems to me, it starts with the relation with Clara. It isn't difficult to notice the change—the change in the writing—that begins just then. The characterisation of Clara has, it seems to me, a certain functional quality—she is a function in the growth of another rather than a person in herself—and this is a world away from all the earlier people. We can see on reflection why this was always likely. At certain critical points of adolescence and growth people do become functions—can be seen as functions—of another's development. It doesn't last; it can't, in any real life. In its very character as a function it is a means of release but often no more than that; not a relationship in itself. Still the difficulty indicates something that Lawrence had to face, of a new kind: not the flow of life, at once personal and social, but growth, change, under real pressures—adult pressures; decisive new relationships; a working self-defining world. A different way of seeing, a different way of writing.

We can only go on to define those new ways if we remember the earlier writing; remember what kind of life, what kinds of relationship, it so finely embodies. Lawrence's crisis—it's not hard to see—is a crisis of separation. But then we at once have to say that the separation was not willed, it came out of that earlier life. Still, to write of separation, as George Eliot and Hardy had found, proposes quite new problems in the novel as a form.

It's hard to express this because of course we've been formed, to an important extent, by the whole process that Lawrence lived through and was writing. We think of it through that formation in quite static ways, often. Separation—individuality. Community—togetherness. All the feelings, all the difficulties are in those awkward translations (and translation of course can start from either language, either feeling). But what I mean by the effect on form is that while a writer can take for granted or can learn to compose some actual community (it can vary very much in its social details) then his persons are there, are given; are there (does it seem paradoxical?) *as themselves* in certain irreducible ways. Not selected persons, not persons composed in a single life's trajectory or around an idea or a theme; but there in the way neighbours are, friends are, the people we work with are. The members of a family offer the simplest example of all.

Now it isn't just a question of how far these people are knowable. It precedes that. It's simply that before they are or mean anything else they are quite radically present; as I said, irreducible. And in fact it's one of Lawrence's deepest emphases that we need to know (that wouldn't be his word: sense, acknowledge), that we need to recognise other people in just this irre-

ducible quality, quite before they are functions or influences
or social or personal roles in our lives. I don't at all mean, by
the way, that these are 'pre-social' selves. I mean that they are
there quite apart from though of course connected to our own
observing existence. While that community holds, the reality
of other people (we must risk and even insist on saying) is in
this sense *given*. And the novel itself is then composed from this
level: not always actual people of course (though Lawrence
started there significantly often) but people conceived in that
way, as irreducibly present in and as themselves. And it's one
of the paradoxes of the literature of developed individualism
that in a later mode this is never really so; never so for others.
A quite radical, recognisable, irreducible presence is reserved
in this later mode for oneself.

Now this way of putting it seems to me the only critical
question that matters about *The Rainbow* and *Women in Love*.
Indeed the remarkable thing about *The Rainbow* is that in its
very form it tries to enact this process, but of course, under
pressure, to a willed conclusion. We often quote that sentence
from the 1914 letter to Edward Garnett:

> You mustn't look in my novel for the old stable *ego* of the
> character.

And we fit that in with an argument for the 'psychological'
novel, as opposed to the 'social'. It's not really that at all.
Compare what I was just saying about the irreducible reality
of people—that sense of community, of an experience of community—with what Lawrence says earlier in that letter, in that
critical year:

> I don't so much care about what the woman *feels*—in the ordinary
> usage of the word. That presumes an *ego* to feel with. I only care
> about what the woman *is*.

It's significant of course that he goes on to define this as 'what
she *is* as a phenomenon'. Enough of his earlier sense, a given

reality, remains to direct the emphasis but also it is already problematical enough to require definition in other terms: 'inhuman, physiological, material'—in that sense already profoundly alien. What he is struggling to define is a process in which

> there is another *ego*, according to whose action the individual is unrecognisable.

Instead of following the lines of known—stable—characters, his novel will compose its characters, its states of being, in 'some other rhythmic form'.

What is that form? In *The Rainbow* I think it is the experience of community as I've been trying to define it, and then of its breakdown. The given reality of men and women is the experience and the method of the early chapters, and then under pressure—the pressures of altering ways of life, economic and social and physical changes—such a reality, radical and irreducible, has to be made or found; it is not given. It is then made and found—attempted to be made and found—in certain kinds of relationship: physical certainly but physical mainly as a discovery of being, of spirit. Other people drop away. They become increasingly irrelevant to this intense and desperate effort. Just because the reality is no longer given—and that loss is explicit; a social system, industrialism, has destroyed given reality by forcing people into systematic roles—the new reality, that which in its turn is irreducible and radical, has to be fought for—the strain and the violence are obvious. It has to be grasped, wrought, celebrated; consciously celebrated even when its real processes are shown as unconscious.

The language of this Lawrence—the Lawrence of this reality —is then necessarily different from the earlier language. It is not the flow with others: a place, a shared language. It is self-generated; making and insisting on its own rhythms, its own terms. The fifteenth chapter of *The Rainbow*, 'The Bitterness of

Ecstasy', shows this change completely: from the language of community—Ursula looking around her, using 'ordinary tools'—through the language of ideas—the critical transition through the microscope, seeing 'incalculable physical and chemical activities'—to the received emotional language, only a slight development from the conventionally romantic—'she loved him, the body of him, whatever his decisions might be'—and finally to 'the fight, the struggle for consummation' and 'the salt bitter passion of the sea, indifferent to the earth, its swinging, definite motion, its strength, its attack, and its salt burning'.

In *The Rainbow* this process is active throughout. The range of reality is persistently tested and explored. The importance of *Women in Love* is that it is a kind of conclusion. The novel is composed from the beginning in a different sense. It is remarkable of course, and one keeps going back to it. But it is necessary to insist that it is not a climax. It is a particular formation at that stage of the difficulty. And I don't myself take it as ratifying. We can't stop at seeing what it expresses; seeing and recommending. We need also to look at what it is, what its form is, what actual reality it composes.

Women in Love, we can say, is a radical *simplification* of the novel, in the interest of a single important emphasis. The concentration on isolated relationships, the dropping of other people and of the texture of ordinary life as irrelevant, had in *The Rainbow* been simply the climax of a history. Here it is a whole and separate form: crystalline certainly, with its own loveliness and intensity of structure; but effectively precipitated not only from an ordinary fictional world but from the community of experience which he had earlier been writing. I don't want to deny, I would prefer to emphasise what Lawrence can then discover in radical experience: at the very roots of being. But at this height of his powers he is being pulled both ways:

towards what is really a kind of dissolution, yet through it to a
hardening abstract form. Effective community has gone. This
is the fiction not only of an isolated but of an essentially random
and transitory group. But not personal experience in place of
social experience. On the contrary, personal experience itself
narrowed down to a single generation: the parents, the past,
the known place left behind as irrelevant; the children, the
future, any kind of settlement in their turn inconceivable.
Between an irrelevant past and an inconceivable future ('the
mystery could dispense with man') what is then known as
personal life is in its different ways 'not enough'. Beyond such
relationships is now a wished-for 'singleness', 'pure single
being', 'the pure duality of polarisation, each one free from
any contamination of the other', or that 'perfection of the
polarised sex-circuit' which in its very isolation, its barrenness,
limits any available fulfilment. And while the isolated relationships are a struggle for something beyond this, for direct relation with the 'non-human mystery', they are either openly
destructive (Gudrun, Gerald, Loerke)—'mystic knowledge in
disintegration and dissolution'; 'ice-destructive knowledge,
snow-abstract annihilation'—or they are resigned, wary, dis-
appointed (Birkin, Ursula) at the edge of what is 'so merely
human'.

Lawrence exerts all his powers to face this experience, which
is in its own way an ending. But hardening through his exploration is this new abstract form. In writing *The Rainbow* he
had wanted to get away from 'the moral scheme into which all
the characters fit', and he realised with the perception of genius
that this would be primarily a change in the form of the novel,
at that deciding level at which reality is composed. It is then
very significant that *Women in Love*, more clearly than any of
his earlier novels, has 'a moral scheme into which all the
characters fit'. It is his own scheme certainly (though with

direct relations to the crisis—the social-and-personal crisis—of
the turn of the century). In so far as he was simply objecting to
an old morality (as in his prolonged and very personal
struggle with the Tolstoy of *Anna Karenina*, which underlies
Women in Love and is explicit, even formal, in *Lady Chatterley's
Lover*) he had of course come through. But in the act of isolation—in the removal of his characters from an actual society,
replacing direct relations with reactions to what had been left
behind; in the reduction to a single generation, so that feelings
are not actions and consequences but must compose their own
pseudo-active world; in the abandonment of place so that the
material and social world is now a landscape, a projected landscape, of alternative states of being—in these acts of isolation
he had composed a new kind of novel. It is an original and
deeply influential kind but it has a scheme and rigidities as hard
as any he had begun by rejecting. Reality is now composed,
under these terrible pressures, from the scheme outwards: at
the level, that is, of the seized organisation. In particular perceptions, particular scenes, *Women in Love* is an exploration, a
creation, of a unique kind. But its organisation is increasingly
isolated and determined. It is not in any way surprising that
after this for nearly ten years Lawrence's best work is in stories,
short stories, where the exploration could hold, and that the
novels of this period—*The Plumed Serpent* is the clearest
example—are for all their energy willed and abstract: the only
form of an extensive kind still available to his imagination.

It could be said of course that *Women in Love* is the last stage
before this: the last successful long work. In many ways this is
true. It has a radical life in it at very many points. But the best
evidence that it belongs to a period before the split—before the
pulling apart of direct response to being and the need for an
abstract scheme—is that at some crucial points and especially in
the ending it is inconclusive. Indeed the inconclusiveness, as of

the final paragraph, is the most redeeming sign. What he is writing more powerfully than any English novelist of the century is the experience of loss: a loss of what, in writing, he had himself found—the experience of community, of the irreducible reality of himself and other human beings. *Women in Love* is a masterpiece of loss, and it enacts this loss in itself. He hesitated, significantly, about how it should end; how it could end. In one possible ending which he later wrote as the play *Touch and Go* he imagined the return: taking the experience back to the broken struggling community in which its real roots lay. It does not succeed, that imagined return, but the impulse is important. It is the essential connection to *Lady Chatterley's Lover*, where the alternative drafts are again significant: the social identity of Mellors being the characteristic difficulty: the condition, the working condition, what possible working condition, for that kind of radical renewal, the touch, the experience, the reality of others?

In an essay on Galsworthy, written while he was composing *Lady Chatterley's Lover*, Lawrence wrote something that has been quoted very often, but with only part of its significance emphasised.

> When the human being becomes too much divided between his subjective and objective consciousness, at last something splits in him and he becomes a social being. When he becomes too much aware of objective reality, and of his own isolation in the face of a universe of objective reality, the core of his identity splits, his nucleus collapses, his innocence or his naiveté perishes, and he becomes only a subjective-objective reality, a divided thing hinged together but not strictly individual.

'Too much aware of objective reality': that of course has been used repeatedly to define a kind of fictional materialism—indeed just Galsworthy's world. But there is something else: 'too much aware of his own isolation in the face of a universe

of objective reality'. That hasn't to do with Galsworthy, but
with Lawrence himself. It is where he had got to, in *Women in
Love*. What he called a 'naive at-oneness with the living
universe' had gone, had been ragged: by education and by
class; by war and struggle, the deformities of poverty and
power; by the abstract definitions, pro and anti, 'endlessly
talking'. It had to be desperately fought back to; abstractly and
stiltedly defined; ritually and hypnotically invoked. 'A divided
thing hinged together'. That is not kind or meant to be kind. For
it is a writer of genius at the farthest point of his insight; a condition to face, to live through, but never, never at all, to ratify.

What he never quite finished in *Women in Love*, what he
could not finish in that final but not concluding isolated crisis,
he now takes up again. He takes it back, still hesitantly, to the
place where the identity had been lost. Instead of staring, coldly
and resignedly, at the figures of loss, he sets out to find how
what he now calls the flame can be kept alive in an ugly and
divided and rootless society. This is reaching significantly
beyond the celebration of 'proud singleness' or the disappoint-
ment in what is 'so merely *human*'. It is flame, touch, recognition, discovery; a search again, at the last, for what is irreducible, substantial, life-bearing in others and in another. It is
trying to find how to grow in an actual society; to keep not
only the flame but a child alive, a recreated family alive, in a
using repressive world. The difficulties are obvious: in the
naming, often the compulsive naming of the physical realities
through which the recognition must come; a defiant naming,
that has to be naming because the threat is so close, the flame
itself so nearly out.

There's no simple judgment. It can be a healing naming, a
naming of love; or a compulsive anxious repetition, trying to
talk the flame back. But it's very significant that he goes back,
goes home, in this last of his novels, to the ordinary words, the

ordinary English words; back where the feeling still was, where the life still was. I mean if we had to choose between that ordinary naming—the names we all know, that are there shared between us—and the private rhetoric, the invented and abstract symbolic language of the more critical fiction: if we had to choose between these I don't know how it would go but I know how it would go for me: to where speech is, where community is; even and especially this suppressed repressed community; the words we learn from others and speak to ourselves and through the difficulties of growth then hesitantly again to others: the words of an experience, an irreducible reality, that an impoverished community, an unfulfilled community, has formally and anxiously to reject, to push down.

Lady Chatterley's Lover hasn't the scale, the sustenance, of the earlier novels. In its single and powerful dimension it is still isolated, still reduced, from the form that had once seemed possible. But it is a positive flow again, a recovery of energy, a reaching past rigidities, and as such very moving. That he was still to the end reaching out, reaching out as a novelist, is profoundly encouraging. It is what we remember and stick to in and through the difficulties—the common difficulties—which his development of the novel, his unfinished development, show us so very clearly. Because it isn't after all an end with Lawrence. It is where in our time we have had to begin.

CONCLUSION

IT is now about forty years since that last novel of Lawrence's. Forty years from that to the centre of Hardy, forty years back again to Dickens and those months of 1847 and 1848. The sense of time is strange, often, in literature and in history. If I say I can feel a direct continuity with this work and experience I've been tracing I don't mean at all that nothing has happened since Lawrence, or that the English novel ended there. It's always different, of course, reading the works of one's own adult lifetime, and there's that familiar illusion of history that the past not only is but was much clearer, much more achieved, than the present. And I don't, as it happens, believe in some recent cultural decline, in the novel any more than in other activities. It's easy to feel baffled by the insistent multiplicity of the present and there's always the temptation of making long-term adjustments to short-term difficulties. Most of the talk about the decline of the novel seems to me exactly that.

But I was following, you'll remember, a particular bearing, and I didn't claim through those earlier decades and the many thousands of available novels to be mapping the whole ground. The works and the experiences I tried to describe were selected in a very simple sense—that there had to be selection in any-thing other than a catalogue—but also and frankly in a more complex sense: that along this particular bearing we could now connect and continue. And this is in any case what I under-stand by tradition. It isn't something handed to us, handed down. What's handed down with some weight is an establish-ment, and in every creative generation one of the first jobs is getting rid of those connections and then of course finding others. Any important tradition is selective, not only the usual bulk-sorting but selective in the precise sense that we take the meanings—and not only the achieved meanings; also if we are serious the difficulties—that we feel and discover we need.

And it's in this sense I'm saying I feel a direct continuity with these works and experiences I've emphasised. I think the problems of community and specifically, in the novel, of the knowable community are still close and difficult, and that whatever we may do in other directions we are still driven, necessarily, to what is possible in that area in the way of creative response. I don't think, that is to say, that these problems are too far back. Indeed when I think back to *Lady Chatterley's Lover* in 1928 and to the General Strike only two years earlier I know there are connections of the most imperative kind. Every middle-aged generation, through its official spokesmen, announces that the world has changed since its young days. Every young generation—and here with more point, for no real life has precedents—announces a beginning.

But then as our actual life takes shape—I mean a shape in experience and not in what is supposed to have happened—certain creative connections, certain significant bearings come to run from the present to the past. In the official history, everything has changed, since the end of Empire, or since the war in 1914: those versions of the modern that are now generally current. But we discover our epoch, as Balzac or Dickens or George Eliot discovered it, not by the generalities of period but by those points, those lives, those experiences, in which the structure of our own most significant difficulties seems to begin to take shape. Never as models of course. The very awareness of continuity makes any concept of models irrelevant. It is an active history not a series of precedents. But we go with attention where the experience has led us before we thought about history. And in my own case I go, on this particular bearing, to the problem of knowable community. A problem that isn't just community as an isolable word, but that involves, as I've argued, basic questions of relationship, of knowing ourselves and others, ourselves with others, under very specific and active and continuing pressures.

What I found on that bearing in the novels I've already tried to say: incompletely but not, I hope, tentatively; in a number of ways on an edge. And I could go on now to follow the bearings after Lawrence, in the work that interests me: much of it, as it happens, in other literatures, and those connections, in their different ways, of course also run back. I could follow Lawrence to Grassic Gibbon in *A Scots Quair*, which I came to very late but which I'm sure is important; or that earlier Lawrence, English Lawrence, to Alan Sillitoe and David Storey and the edge—the narrower, more jagged edge, that I certainly feel there. After Conrad, but more often I'm afraid after Kipling, there's been a very lively literature, sea-crossing literature, in the experience of imperialism, the experience our way round: Joyce Cary's African novels, early Orwell, and in the late colonial wars Graham Greene. Where Wells got to at the peak of his writing, Orwell also followed in those novels of the 1930s, and of course Utopia got its negatives—its period negatives, now fading I think, in Huxley and in Orwell and in Golding. There is still a country house, little changed from before the first war, with Ivy Compton-Burnett in a kind of scrupulous residence, and there've been a few surprising new tenants, going steadily up in the world, whose names I've heard but for the moment have forgotten. While as for being alone in the city, there are so many now alone there, right down to copywriters, that I live in hopes they may even one day bump into and meet each other; even start to acknowledge a social condition. But what's more usually acknowledged, even by the copywriters, is what's called a human condition—as good an excuse as any for not meeting. And while that lasts, in now portentous single voices, a city of eight million people goes about its business and is even, as that, beginning to be noticed.

The fiction of special pleading: well it's changed its sex, or so it seemed recently: a persuasive first-person insinuation, that got called anger but keeps changing its accents, finding its position (but this was always predictable) comfortable. But still beyond all this, in the most difficult, least absorbable, least nameable work, the problems of knowable community, in so many different ways. Joyce Cary and Angus Wilson: very deeply committed, continually experimenting writers. And the sense of experiment is the whole point. It can't be done, that exploration, in a single ratifying explaining voice. In so profound and so difficult a multipersonal reality, the shapes of observation can seem to turn to shadows, and the grammar of presentation, of contemporary presentation, is very difficult to learn.

I see two critical bearings: the problem of analysis, now necessarily social, which has been exceptionally difficult in a long period of compromise (for there is no analysis in consensus); and the problem of that extended and still rapidly mobile society, in which the lives of a majority of our people are still for the most part ignored or at best visited. When I say that the problems including the formal problems of the novel are in the end mainly problems of relationships I am pointing to an area where it is still difficult to relate, a continuing and more general experience of the conflict of the educated and the customary. And not only superficially, but deep in the language, deep in the feelings, deep—it is now clear—in the forms.

'Begin' Virginia Woolf said ironically:

Begin by saying that her father kept a shop in Harrogate. Ascertain the rent. Ascertain the wages of shop assistants in 1878.

Discover what her mother died of. Describe cancer. Describe calico. Describe . . .

And I can remember very well when to read that out in Cambridge would be to find assent, a ripple of assent, in the quite familiar certainty that we had better things to do. I don't find this now. Perhaps I don't meet the right people. But 'describe cancer, describe calico'. One of these at least we still have to describe, and we have other means of knowing the wages of shop assistants than that faintly comic ascertaining. We know what she was offering instead, of course.

Examine for a moment an ordinary mind on an ordinary day. The mind receives a myriad impressions—trivial, fantastic, evanescent, or engraved with the sharpness of steel. From all sides they come, an incessant shower of innumerable atoms.

And we have had that fiction: not a series of gig lamps (and of course we can do without them) but the 'luminous halo', the 'semi-transparent envelope', and then of course it depends who's wearing it or who posted it, materialising as it does with 'no plot, no comedy, no tragedy, no love-interest or catastrophe in the accepted style'. It's a wise reservation, that 'accepted style', but there's one translation of the method—a relevant translation—as 'no people'. And we have to say in any case that 'the ordinary mind on an ordinary day' is social, that it relates us necessarily to others, and that consciousness, real consciousness, doesn't come passively like that, a receiving of impressions, but is what we learn, what we make, in our real relationships including with fathers and mothers and shops.

But then see why the impulse comes, why it still comes strongly though in a different mode and even in some new waves. So much more of life, it can seem to many, is now incorporated, processed, perpetually informed and communicated. It can seem a reasonable strategy to continue the novel by a kind of negative definition: what the other media are not, or more generally what the public world doesn't bother, doesn't know enough, to report. Very few of us live as now most of us read. I mean as having parts, consciousness, in that official and daily history. And the phrases are waiting, as I argued earlier: *that* life is public, social, sociological: *this* life that matters is personal, private—the semi-transparent envelope as opposed, dramatically opposed, to the headline.

And of course since the disjunction is there many intense experiences, with just that location and emphasis, come to nourish and continue the novel. I wouldn't argue against them, I read many with respect. All I'd go on to say is that the disjunction itself—where the two worlds seem to break but where in regular experience they of course interact, and more than interact: combine, fuse—needs our direct and very serious attention. The impulse to leave the most general alone is a learned impulse, even a trained impulse. Or to leave it alone in the novel: write it as sociology, even as criticism. It's not for me to argue against these later modes. They have their substantial uses and for the last thirty years there's been an interesting and maybe fruitful confusion of forms, between imaginative work and those other accounts. Some important writers move from one to the other, in one to the other; Orwell is only the first example. And yet it remains true, looking at it from experience, that there are certain feelings, certain relationships, certain fusions and as relevantly certain dislocations, which can only be conceived in the novel, which indeed demand the novel and in just this difficult border country where from Dickens to Lawrence, making its own very varied demands, it has lived and lived with meaning.

Of course one thing has changed, since that generation of the 1840s. The novel isn't any longer the unchallenged dominant form. The drama has come back with great power in some significant areas, and it has, we must remember, many inherent powers to present, a multipersonal reality. The rise of the film has been very like the earlier rise of the novel: a dominant popular mode with very great creative powers, though its creative difficulties have been very similar—are now particularly similar—to the creative difficulties, difficulties of relationships and consciousness, of the novel. You'll also have noticed, I expect, an obvious similarity between serial fiction and television serials, and it still sometimes surprises me that they're still regularly put (rightly on a lot of the evidence) at a level below possibility, I mean below the possibility of connection, and of creation rather than simple reproduction. All these changes are affecting the novel, the possibilities and place of the novel, but still to understand art is to know there's no competition in that market sense. The experience finds, makes its form; and for many of us, more than enough of us, that's still, and I'm glad, the novel; and the novel here in this country, in this society we've been tracing.

It is a history then, from Dickens to Lawrence, to give us courage; not precedents but meanings, connecting meanings. And it is significantly a history that isn't otherwise recorded: part of the history of a people which if these novels weren't written would be decidedly, demonstrably, inadequate. What we are told of the history of ideas and of the general history of the society is different, looks different, when these novels have been read. That sense of the problematic, in community and identity, in knowable relationships, is more deeply there and is earlier there than anywhere else in our recorded experience.

For I haven't been saying, have never wanted to say, that the society—this unprecedented dislocating mobile society— produced the novels. It doesn't happen like that. Society, what is called society, is the composed account, and to any composed account you can of course fit a superstructure. But while society is lived, while it is being lived, the novel, these novels, are in the nerves, the bloodstream, the living fibres of its experience. In any living society this miracle is enacted (what in a degraded philosophy, a degraded aesthetic, can seem only a miracle): that a unique life, in a place and a time, speaks from its own uniqueness and yet speaks a common experience; speaks in a work in language, in a common language, that in its shaping becomes its own but is still common, still connects with others.

Much ordinary social experience is of course directly reflected, represented, in what is indeed an ideology, what can be called a superstructure. But in any society at all like our own, and especially in this one this last hundred and fifty years, there's a very vital area of social experience—*social* experience— that doesn't get incorporated: that's neglected, ignored, certainly at times repressed; that even when it's taken up, to be processed or to function as an official consciousness, is resistant, lively, still goes its own way, and eventually steps on its shadow—steps, I mean, in such a way that we can see which is shadow and which substance.

It is from this vital area, from this structure of feeling that is lived and experienced but not yet quite arranged as institutions and ideas, from this common and inalienable life that I think all art is made. And especially these novels, these connecting novels, which come through to where we are just because all that life, that unacknowledged life now so movingly shaped and told, is our own direct and specific and still challenging inheritance.

Index